FATHER
JOE

*A Year of Wit,
Wisdom & Warmth*

FATHER
JOE

A Year of Wit,
Wisdom & Warmth

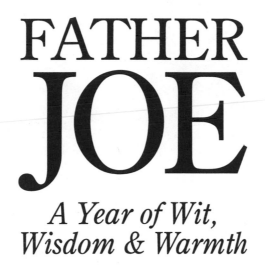

Father Joseph Breighner

Cathedral Foundation Press
Baltimore, Maryland

Published by
Cathedral Foundation Press
P.O. Box 777
Baltimore, Maryland 21203

Manufactured in the United States of America

Edited by Judith M. Ciofalo
Cover Photograph by Denise Walker
Cover and Book Design by James A. Morrisard

ISBN 1-885938-00-4

Library of Congress Catalog Card Number: 94-68116

All articles in this book were published
with permission from *The Catholic Review*

Introduction

Shortly after I was named editor of *The Catholic Review*, a little more than eight years ago, I began tinkering with ways to improve the newspaper. I was warned that whatever I did, don't change Father Joe Breighner's column. He has a loyal, and vocal, following. Well, on rare occasion Father Breighner's column didn't get published in the newspaper. Then the phones would start ringing. It got to the point where the office secretary warned me that if I didn't publish Father Breighner every week, I'd have to answer all the phones myself. That's why I'm especially pleased that Cathedral Foundation Press is publishing this collection of Father Joe's columns. Because if for reasons beyond my control his column doesn't appear in *The Catholic Review*, I can direct his fans to a chapter in his book.

It's a pleasure to be Father Joe's editor. To many readers of his newspaper column, Father Joe is as comforting as a weekly visit from a parish priest. Through his *Country Roads* radio show, which is carried coast to coast, he has developed the same ardent following.

I've tried to identify the source of Fr. Joe's popularity. Discerning readers may know it instinctively but I've come up with four reasons why Father Joe is such a consistent, comforting columnist.

Certainly, Father Joe is familiar. Having written a newspaper column for more than 20 years, Father Joe is a steady voice, promoting the Christian message in a troubled world. With more than two decades of weekly columns behind him, he is certainly a dean among Catholic newspaper columnists and he may be achieving elder statesman status among all newspaper columnists. And no matter the issue, no matter the complexity, Father Joe brings the reader back to the central point of life: God's everlasting love and the promise of salvation.

Father Joe is prophetic. In his writings he announces, laments, encourages, chastises and amuses. Sometimes he does all of that within the span of 650 words. Father Joe brings Catholicism to real life issues. He's written thoughtfully on everything from biomedical ethics to baseball. And miraculously, Father Joe has found God there waiting for him and his readers.

Father Joe is a master storyteller. He has a unique way of presenting a downhome, everyday spirituality. His stories are human and divine where the ordinary and the extraordinary mix easily with homespun wisdom and celestial revelation. For example, everyone can identify with Father Joe's observation that "no one ever said on their deathbed, 'I wish I had cleaned more.'" He personalizes faith and makes the greatest mysteries of life a comforting, everyday experience.

Finally, Father Joe is genuine. The Father Joe you read is the same Father Joe you meet. This collection of his columns is a year's worth of entertainment. More importantly, it's a lifetime's worth of inspiration.

In this book, several of his major themes are grouped by subject so the reader can follow one theme or select from a potpourri of short pieces sampling Father Joe's wit, wisdom and warmth. Easy to read, easy to understand, every piece in this book invites the reader to pause and reflect. And in this fast-paced-information-superhighway-fax-a-moment world, any invitation to quiet thoughtfulness is a moment to treasure.

Daniel Medinger
August, 1994

Foreword

Over the years, in writing sermons, weekly columns, and radio scripts (not to mention other talks for workshops, days of recollection and parish missions) I am often asked, "Where do you get your ideas?" While I obviously do continued extensive study and reading, my most honest answer is usually, "From God!" Years ago, when I first began my ministry, I always had the sense that, when I began writing, something else was happening, and someone else was taking over. Ideas began to flow that didn't seem to come from me. Thoughts materialized that I had not formulated. Insights occurred that seemed to come from outside myself. It was then that I realized that I felt closest to God when I was writing.

My favorite self-description is that I'm "God's scribe." The prayer I most often say before I begin writing is "Lord, what do you want me to tell your people." The blessing I most often pray on my writing is "Lord, may your words be mine, and may my words be yours."

Now, lest a loud voice from heaven speak out and say, "Hey, Breighner, don't blame me for all of your writings!" let me quickly add that the "best" of my writings I credit to God, The "other" writings are the result of my not hearing too well or God not speaking loud enough.

This book is one effort to compile the "best" of my *Catholic Review* columns. It would not exist without the efforts of Dan Medinger, the editor of the *Review*, or Andy Ciofalo or James Morrisard. It would not exist without the weekly inspiration of Jackie Grey, or the lifetime inspiration of my sister Helen or the eternal patience of God.

So I thank all of them, and most especially, I thank the many readers over the years who kept encouraging me with comments like "I never miss your column" or "I have your columns all over my refrigerator door" or "You write in a way that the average person can understand. You take complicated topics and make them easier to comprehend." So I dedicate this book to those faithful weekly readers who made it possible for another group of readers to share these reflections.

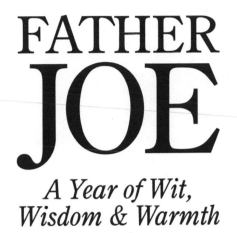

FATHER
JOE

A Year of Wit,
Wisdom & Warmth

To Helen and Mike

JANUARY

On To Heaven
and Higher

■

    In these early weeks of the New Year, I recall a wonderful Jewish tale that is often told near Rosh Hashana, the beginning of the Jewish new year.

    As the story goes, there was a small town in Lithuania years ago named Nemirov. There lived a rabbi there who was thought to be the holiest man in the universe. It was said that each year before Rosh Hashana the rabbi was lifted up to heaven to talk with God.

    Everyone agreed that this was so, except for one man. That one man was the Litvak, a born doubter. He believed only in what he could see, and the rabbi looked like an ordinary man to him. So he decided to follow the rabbi on new year's morning.

    He watched the rabbi get up, dress in a plain woodsman's outfit and go into the forest. There he saw the rabbi chop down a tree, split the trunk into logs and sticks and then carry them away.

    He followed the rabbi as he went to the home of a poor bedridden widow. The rabbi knocked, greeted the widow, offered her the wood free of charge, built her a roaring fire in her fireplace, said his prayers and then left.

    The story concludes that the Litvak remained in Nemirov forever after and became one of the rabbi's most faithful followers. When anyone in the town would tell the stranger how their rabbi went to heaven to see God right before the new year, he would reply, "Yes, he does go to heaven and even higher."

In harsh economic times with threats of war around us, I think we need to remember gentle stories like that. I believe that Jesus said, "Blessed are the meek, they shall inherit the earth," because he realized only the meek understand the earth.

After armies have marched and kingdoms have been toppled and new flags have been raised, the meek will still be here.

They will be the first to suffer from wars and economic hard times, but they will also be the first to repair the damage and bind up wounds. Armies are finished when the enemy has been slain or conquered, but the meek are finished only when everyone learns to love one another.

After wars are fought and tragedies occur, Catholic Relief Services and the Red Cross and other humanitarian organizations will move in with aid. Might the world not be better if we first invaded other countries with armies of meek and loving people who come only to bring medicine and healing and comfort?

No, I'm not a pacifist. I'm glad that there are police officers on the street to keep us from getting mugged and robbed just as there must be armies in the world to protect us from global tyrants. People not controlled by love must at least be restrained by force. Yet, while I recognize the necessity of strength to control the violent, I also recognize that only love brings change. To reverse that sentence, it will also take a lot of change before love can control us.

That's why I love the story of the rabbi. The part of the globe we can control is the part of the globe we live on.

In an interview, Barbara Bush once said, "I believe that what goes on in your house is more important than what goes on in the White House." Barbara Bush lived in the White House and believes that. I've never been to the White House, and I believe that.

This does not mean that we just focus on "our own" and too bad for the rest of the world. Rather it means that we love our families and neighbors and teach by example to extend love beyond the family and beyond the neighborhood.

In a violent world, we need to rediscover the nonviolence of love. We need to do the good deed that no one sees, to offer the help that no one but the recipient knows about, to care for someone and something beyond ourselves.

Too many of us live in hope of arriving in heaven some day and forget that we can go beyond heaven every day. To see God in every person we meet, to serve God in every hurting person we encounter is, indeed, to go to heaven and even higher.

Put a Positive Spin on the New Year

New Year's resolutions often amount to nothing more than an exercise in wishful thinking. Instead, may I suggest this new year that we make specific decisions to perform specific activities. Here are two categories: first, loving God and neighbor, and second, loving ourselves.

To make sure that we love God each day, let me reaffirm some ideas, specifically how five minutes a day can change our lives.

First, begin and end each day in prayer. Upon arising, first thing each morning say, "Thank you, Lord, for today. Please stay with me today, Lord." Then say an Our Father, a Hail Mary and a Glory Be.

You can do this while kneeling, standing, shaving, showering: The body position is not as important as the inner disposition. Begin the day talking to God.

Second, end the day similarly. At the end of the day say, "Thank you, Lord, for today. Bless what was good. Please forgive what needs forgiving." Then another Our Father, Hail Mary and Glory Be. Again, the position of the body is not as important as the disposition of the heart.

You have begun and ended the day in prayer. In between, take some time during each day to do something that helps someone else.

That may involve something as small as letting someone else into a line of traffic, holding a door for someone, smiling at a salesperson, being pleasant with co-workers or picking a piece of paper off the ground and throwing it away.

It may involve something as big as visiting a funeral home or a hospital, sending a note of comfort or congratulations. Make it a point to do something every day that makes someone else's life a little easier.

Between prayer and your "good deed" that means about five minutes a day to express love of God and neighbor.

Unfortunately, though Jesus said to "love your neighbor as yourself," I think we often forget to love ourselves. Allow me to suggest something you can do for yourself at the beginning of each day that can literally revolutionize your life.

Resolve every day of the new year to begin each day by asking yourself these five questions:

- What do I have to be grateful for today? Name two things: health, home, family, faith, job. Begin with gratitude.

- Who is there that makes me feel loved? Name two people: spouse, sister, brother, friend, neighbor, parent, grandparent.

- What excites me about today? Name at least two things: a day to learn, to help someone, to make the world better, to see a sunrise or sunset, etc.

- What energizes me about today? Name two things: How can I make work or school more fun today? How can I enjoy things I often miss – trees, flowers, snow, rain, etc. How can I find something today that excites me?

- What special gift will God give me today? Allow yourself to imagine that God has something nice for you today, if you only notice – like a beautiful sky, a nice compliment, a sense of accomplishment, a bargain, a raise, etc.

Do you get the point of these questions? They are to help us change our focus from what's wrong or bad with life to what is good and exciting and special about life.

If we begin each day with negative questions like "Why do I have to get up?" or "Why do I have to do this?" then we set ourselves up for a bad day.

But if we can turn it around and say, "Today I have the opportunity to work. I have a chance to be a good parent today. I have a chance to be a good spouse or friend or neighbor."

In short, if we change the questions we ask ourselves, we change how we view life and ultimately, how we live life.

If we can move from the wishful thinking of general resolutions to the specific decision to follow new behaviors, then we will not just have to wish a happy new year. We will have taken steps to make it happy.

Learning From
an Old Dog

In a new year, what can we learn from an old dog?

For so long we have repeated the adage "You can't teach an old dog new tricks." A better question, however, might be "Can an old dog teach us new tricks?"

On a retreat recently, as I returned from a walk in the West Virginia woods, I spotted an old dog near the retreat house. He was a large black dog – how else would a dog dress at a place called Priestfield? – and looked something like a Labrador, but mostly he looked like a mutt.

As he rose to his feet, he stretched his arthritic limbs gingerly and awkwardly walked toward me, wagging his tail slightly to assure me that I was not a potential menu item.

Being a lifetime dog lover, I petted him and started scratching his back. The way to a man's heart may be his stomach, but the way to a dog's heart is definitely by the back scratch. As he luxuriated in the scratching, his nose pointing to the sky, he seemed to come alive.

Playfully, he started looking around, spotted a stick nearby and gingerly trotted over to it. Picking it up in his mouth, he started back toward me. No doubt some old script from puppyhood days was playing in his mind.

To my surprise, however, he walked right past me with the stick and at a safe distance sat down.

Still holding the stick, he looked at me triumphantly as if to say, "Hey, in my puppy days, I would have brought the stick to you and you would have thrown it and I would have chased it. I'm too old for that kind of nonsense. Do you like my version of the game?" An old dog had taught me a new trick.

What's the moral of this parable? Perhaps there are several. First, there is wisdom to old age, even to old dogs. Perhaps our society undervalues that wisdom. With computers and video games and new technology, it remains true that many elderly may have to learn from the young rather than teach the young.

Yet we must never equate technical knowledge with wisdom. With all the new paraphernalia, we would be hard pressed to say that young people are any happier because of it. With all the speed of fax machines and other tools of communication, we seem to have made people more frantic, not more peaceful.

Perhaps those who move more slowly because of age can teach a younger generation about an age when life was slower. We can learn about fidelity, patience, keeping promises, staying faithful in marriage, forgiving others and ourselves, taking time to be courteous and loving and gentle, working hard – even when there are few results to show for it. These are not new tricks. They are old values.

A second moral of the old dog parable is that we can learn to see old things in a new way. Can we learn to pray not trying to get God to do our will but wanting to be peaceful regardless of how things work out?

Can we complement the reverence we show for the Blessed Sacrament by being able to reverence the God who lives in every person we meet?

Believing that bread becomes God is indeed a miracle. Believing that every person we meet is a revelation of God is another miracle. Can we learn to examine our consciences each day, not just counting the sins for which we repent, but also praising God for the goodness we discover?

Our old faith can be continually new if we allow ourselves to look at it with fresh perspective and new eyes.

Finally, wouldn't it be wonderful if you and I treated each other and our God with the faithfulness that an old dog treats a loving owner? Dogs seem to have unconditional love even for those people whom other people find it difficult to love.

Would the world be better if we could see it through the eyes of a dog? Perhaps, especially if we consider that dog spelled backward is God.

God's Authority In a New World Order

■

"When elephants fight, the grass gets hurt."

That African proverb sums up so much of life. When the armed forces of Iraq and the Allies slugged it out, it was the little people who got hurt. The women and children and civilian non-combatants were the victims. The poor are always the first to suffer, and when the mighty have decided who won, the poor will still be poor.

While I am eternally hopeful that people can change, I am not at all optimistic that people will change. The singular figure in history – who came preaching a new way to live, who "taught with authority and not like the scribes" – this figure was crucified. Jesus was done in by the religious authorities who worked in concert with the political authorities in order to use the power of their collective authority to turn the crowds against Jesus.

When elephants plot, the grass gets cut.

In war time, I believe most of us regress psychologically. In the early days of our conflict with Iraq, I can't tell you how many phone calls to radio talk shows went like this: "The government knows more than we do." "I believe the president knows what's best." "We have to trust our leaders." In times of psychological stress and uncertainty, we yield our own wills to a higher authority. We want someone else to take care of us, to tell us what to do, to assure us that what we're doing is the right thing.

Most of the world, it seems to me, is willing to trade freedom for security. We seek strong religious figures who tell us everything from how to be saved to how to raise children. We seek strong governments who will protect our jobs and protect our pensions.

The good thing about strong parental figures is that the young and the weak and the handicapped are protected. The sad thing about giving away our power to authorities though is that we go through life thinking that someone else knows how to run our lives better than we do. As long as we do that we will continue to make elephants of a few people and doom the majority of people to being grass that gets stepped on.

The new world order that President Bush spoke of will simply be a repeat of the old world order if we just replace one dictator with another, substitute one form of power for another and continue to leave most of the world feeling powerless.

What is the answer? I think the new world order must be based on the authority of God.

There's a wonderful line about Jesus in the first chapter of Mark's Gospel. The people are saying of Jesus, "What does this mean? A completely new teaching in a spirit of authority! He gives orders to unclean spirits and they obey him!"

Jesus identified with the poor, the oppressed, the downtrodden, and gave them the power to set themselves free. He gave the power of love.

A new world order can only be based on our collective efforts to come to a new understanding of a God of love. Until we make love the strongest force on earth, the elephants will continue to fight and the grass will continue to hurt.

Fourth Down
and Long

For those who like football but who don't like church, may I ask you to consider what a football team would be without a clubhouse or locker room?

As fans we all would love to see our favorite team run out on the field ready for battle. Seldom do we consider where they come from or go to.

In the clubhouse and locker room, however, is where they get their game plan, their uniforms, their strategy. In other words, in the clubhouse the team gets a sense of direction, an identity and a way to play the game.

At halftime in the middle of the game, both teams return to the locker room. Here if they are winning, they get encouragement to keep it up. If they are losing, they work on a new plan, get a pep talk, find a new way to approach the game.

Perhaps by now you are getting my point. Church is where we come from and go to in order to make sense of life.

In church and religious education, we receive values and commandments and inspiration. We get a game plan for living life. In church we receive our "uniform," our identity in life.

At our baptism and at our funeral we are wrapped in white to symbolize that we live and die as children of God. Our identity influences how we make decisions, how we treat other people, how we cope with tragedy and loneliness and sickness.

A team does not gather in the clubhouse or locker room at the beginning of the season and then not return until the next season. They return before, during and after every game because identity, values and teamwork only come through repetition.

So we gather at church minimally on a weekly basis because we need to keep on being encouraged when things are going well because we need a place to have our spirits boosted when everything we try seems to be going wrong.

Hopefully, the sermon each week is what we need to hear, much as we need to hear different things from a good coach.

Sometimes a little hell needs to be raised, and sometimes peace needs to be preached. Sometimes we need to be comforted, and sometimes we need to be challenged. Just as a coach keeps explaining and interpreting the game book, we need to keep hearing the Good Book.

In a locker room both the victor and the vanquished take time to eat, because each knows that life must go on and the body needs to be nourished. We need to feed on the Bread of Life because if we stop feeding on the Body of Christ, we might just forget that we are the Body of Christ in the world. We need to know that there is life after death, victory after defeat, hope after despair.

Just as locker rooms vary, depending on who won and who lost, so we have feast days as well as funerals. Yet, we all need to gather at church for both, because while there is a time to be happy and a time to mourn, every time is a time for hope.

A locker room can be a smelly place. Dirty socks and sweaty clothes don't win perfume awards! A church too can be a place we bring our dirty laundry, a place where we go to get "cleaned up" through the sacrament of reconciliation. As Ann Landers put it, "The church is not a museum for saints but a hospital for sinners."

We bring our cuts and bruises, not to be condemned or judged, but to be healed, forgiven and sent out again with a new faith in ourselves that comes from a renewed faith in God.

If we are looking for a New Year's resolution, perhaps football offers us one. If players need to keep going to the clubhouse for a sense of direction, an identity, a purpose on the field, so we need to return to church to maintain or rediscover our values, our identity, our purpose in life.

FEBRUARY

Ten Rules for
Loving Yourself

Throughout life we hear much about the love of God and neighbor, but we often don't hear much about the love of self. Yet, Jesus taught us to love our neighbors as our selves, implying that the respect we felt for ourselves would be the respect we would give to others.

Unfortunately, self-love has often been mistaken for selfishness. Nothing could be further from the truth.

Selfishness says, "I look out for me and tough for you." Self-love says, "I learn to value me so that I can more fully love and value you."

Lack of self-love results in untold self-destructive behavior. The alcoholic, the drug addict, the inmate in jail and the abused spouse often share a common problem – they do not love and respect themselves.

Eric Hoffer, the longshoreman/practical philosopher, once wrote, "It is not love of self but hatred of self which is at the root of the troubles that afflict that world."

With this in mind, I have put together what I call the Ten Commandments of Self-Love. I hope these commandments help you to love yourself and, by loving yourself, to more deeply love your neighbor and your God.

TEN COMMANDMENTS OF SELF-LOVE

I
You shall love yourself because your self is a part of God's self.
You have been made in the image and likeness of God.
Love yourself because you are a reflection of God.

II
You shall love yourself even if someone else does not love you.
We humans, because of original sin, can make weak
and fallible judgments. God however is infallible,
and he loves you with an eternal love.

III
You shall love yourself even if you sin.
Guilt is meant to be a reminder of failure, but it is
not a state we are meant to live in. Learning from the past
and changing our attitudes and behaviors rather than
wallowing in guilt make us more like God.

IV
You shall love yourself more than your fear.
Fear will steal life from you. God wants you to have the fullness of
life. Faith is stronger than fear.

V
You shall love yourself in times of despair.
Feelings of despair will pass if we cling to hope in God,
who will last forever.

VI
You shall love yourself enough to give yourself away.
Just as we cannot separate ourselves from God, we cannot
separate our selves from others. As you give to others, so you
give to God and so you act like God.

VII

You shall love yourself because God wants to take on your self.
Just as Jesus took on flesh and blood and was born in Bethlehem
so he wants to take on your flesh and blood and be born in you.
Respect the temple of God that you are.

VIII

You shall love yourself because God is love.
When you love yourself, you give glory to God.

IX

You shall love yourself because God has loved you.
If you were the only person in the world, God would have been
born, suffered and died just for you. If God loves you so,
why would you even dare not to love yourself?

X

You shall love yourself because God wouldn't create a world without you.
God could have chosen to create such a world, but
a world without you just wasn't the kind of world God wanted.
God wants you here. Why would you ever doubt your purpose?

If All God Said Was 'Love Thy Neighbor'

What if that was all we knew?

Suppose that all the bibles and holy books of all the world's religions suddenly disappeared. Suppose that all the priests and ministers and rabbis and religious leaders of different religions did not have different traditions and doctrines to pass on.

Suppose there was only one thing that all people of the world knew about God. What if the only thing we knew for sure about God was that God had communicated a single message to the world, "Love your neighbor as yourself, and you will live forever."?

If that were all we knew about God, would the world be better or worse for it? It would certainly be interesting.

Think how it would affect our image of God. God would be a God of life and love. This would not be a God to be feared, to be ignored, to be placated, to be appeased.

This would just be a God worthy solely of gratitude. Who would not be grateful to a God who only wanted us to love each other and who wanted us to live forever? Imagine the joyous hymns, the exciting rituals, the beautiful stories that would be collected and retold of people who had devoted their lives to living with love.

Think how it would affect our image of other people. We would never kill anyone, thinking God wanted us to do that. There would be no religious persecutions, thinking we ought to force other people to think as we think, to talk as we talk, to worship as we worship, to believe what we believe.

Upon visiting foreign countries and discovering new worlds, our job would not be to subjugate or enslave or change other people or other nations. Our only job would be to love them.

When faced with our interactions with other people on a daily basis, our first presumption would be that cooperating with and helping one another would be far more important than "beating someone else" or getting ahead of someone else.

Think how it would affect my image of myself. I would know that what was important was not how much money I made or how many things I owned or how famous I became. I would know that my sense of self-worth would only come from how much love I shared. My sense of accomplishment at the end of the day would rest on how many other lives I had enriched, how many other people were happier.

While such a thought might be worthy of a book, I'm not so sure that the world might not be better off if all we knew of God is that God said, "Love your neighbor as yourself and you will live forever."

In fact, I'm not so sure that God wanted to say more.

The Truth
About Beauty

A new article on an old theme appeared Feb. 6, 1992, in *The New York Times.* Women basically do not like how they look.

One commentator summed it up this way: "Women are still valued more in the world at large by their looks than men are. What makes such distortions so cruel is that body image and self-esteem are linked. In other words, when we dislike our bodies, it is difficult to like ourselves."

A 1991 survey of 3,000 boys and girls by the American Association of University Women asked them if they were happy. Among white girls in elementary school, 55 percent were happy with themselves; by high school, the percentage had dropped to 22 percent. The study observed, "Up to the age of 11, girls are very straightforward and confident. They trust their own experience and say what they think. By age 12, they're beginning to get mixed messages from their families, the media and society in general that they're supposed to be quiet, nice, thin and preferably blonde."

Studies indicate that young boys, too, struggle with their sense of self-esteem and their body type. In society at large, however, men do not find their value so consistently defined by their weight or their looks.

What is the overall effect of this pressure on women? Naomi Wolf, the author of the "The Beauty Myth" says, "More women have more money and power and scope and legal recognition than we have ever had before. But in terms of how we feel about ourselves physically, we may actually be worse off than our unliberated grandmothers."

What is the antidote for all of this? How can we as a church family help our individual families build up the self-esteem of our young people? Allow me to offer a few suggestions.

First, we need to help our young people and ourselves to learn to look inward for our sense of self-worth rather than outward. In other words we are valuable for what we are rather than for what we do. Jesus said, "The kingdom of God is within you." We are all "created in the image and likeness of God." That image is an essential definition of who we are. It has nothing to do with superficial, accidental qualities of size, weight or hair color.

Not only do we have to teach that external characteristics have nothing to do with our worth, but we have to believe it. One thing belief in God should teach us is that God loves us the way we are and we need to love ourselves the same way.

Second, we adults need to give our young people a lot of praise and reassurance. A wise person said, "Nothing improves our hearing like a compliment." If we think our young people don't listen to us, maybe it's because they are struggling with so much self-criticism within that they can't bear to hear more criticism from the outside. If we could just get in the habit of routinely praising our young people, it would be a wonderful investment in their self-esteem.

Third, we need to tell our young people that society tells lies. Society tells us that we should look a certain way and makes movies and hires models who do look a certain way. We do not have to look a certain way.

The key to all of this is giving our young people a good foundation in self-esteem at an early age. If we do, they will more than likely mature into men and women who do not need to look outside themselves to find inner worth. If we do not build self-esteem from within, then we will continue to be victims of the lies about beauty from without.

Who Will Lift Us Up, If We Keep Dragging Each Other Down?

In the midst of the Gary Hart investigation, a reporter commented, "Everybody agrees that this kind of reporting is terrible, but everyone loves to read it."

We learn a lot about ourselves when we examine what we enjoy. Everyone condemns gossip, but few people can resist listening to it. Confession of our own sins may be declining, but confession of the sins of others seems to be as popular as ever.

Seemingly, next to having our sins forgiven, nothing makes us feel better than knowing that someone else has sinned. Where does this need come from? Apparently, we humans are so insecure about ourselves that we are reassured when we learn that others have failures too. We can say to ourselves, "At least I didn't do that."

Unfortunately as a result, no one comes out ahead. By choosing to drag one another down, we have no one to lift us up. In other words, if we can convince ourselves that everyone is as bad as everyone else, why bother trying to improve?

In absolving ourselves from trying to be saints, we end up with a self-satisfied sense of being a sinner.

The fact of life is that we all are sinners. As Bishop Fulton Sheen once put it, "There is an amazing monotony to human behavior."

All of the great classic writers portrayed their characters with some kind of tragic flaw. Whether it is greed, lust, pride or something else, there is inevitably something that keeps us from being all that we can be. We learn with time that being all we can be invariably includes sin.

What conclusions can we draw from this? Perhaps there are several.

First, if we are all in the same boat, compassion might be a more compelling approach than condemnation. Condemnation might make us feel better, but compassion will make us become better. As I have said before, pain can make us bitter or better. If we allow our failures to make us more forgiving of others, then perhaps we have learned one of life's greatest lessons.

In addition to compassion, our common weakness might also teach us to rely more completely on God. If we learn anything from sin, it is that all of us, on our own, are incapable of resisting it. St. Paul argued in the Scriptures that laws do not keep us from sin. Laws simply tell us when we have sinned. Only Jesus forgives sins, and only his strength can help us to resist sin.

In the Twelve Steps of Alcoholics Anonymous, admitting our helplessness and surrendering to a Higher Power to strengthen us is the first step toward recovery. Our attitude toward anyone else's sins or failures must always be, "There, but for the grace of God, go I." We are not morally superior to other greater sinners. Moral victories do not come from our personal strength but from our openness to allow God to work through us and in us.

Finally, a virtue that we might all pray more for is the virtue of fortitude. To say that God's grace gives us the victory is not to deny the importance of our human choices. We must have the fortitude to do the Christ-like act, even when that may be the last thing we feel like doing.

Character has been defined as "what we are when no one is looking."

Fortitude is the strength to resist evil and to persist in good when every fiber of our being urges us to do the opposite. While fortitude cannot guarantee a victory in every struggle, it can remind us that good is worth struggling for.

Perhaps the Gary Hart saga can become a parable for us. If we become more compassionate, more reliant on God and more appreciative of the virtue of fortitude, then one man's agony has not been in vain.

Ask the Wrong Questions, Get the Wrong Answers

We keep getting the wrong answers because we keep asking the wrong questions.

The question most often asked today is "How do we help keep sexually active young people from getting AIDS?" That usually leads people to the illusory answer of "safe sex."

A better question that might be asked is "How do we help keep young people from having sex indiscriminately?" That leads to the possibility of "save sex."

Save sex until marriage. Save sex, at least, until you are in a committed faithful relationship with one person. Save sex until you are able to be physically, emotionally, spiritually and financially responsible for your partner, your child and yourself.

Those who argue against the possibility of "save sex" insult young people's intelligence. I hear such people argue that the young "are going to do it anyway" as if abstinence is impossible.

Our young people will continue to think abstinence from sex is impossible only as long as we adults keep presuming it's impossible for them and only as long as we don't expect abstinence from them.

On what grounds can we argue for "save sex?" Moral and religious grounds are the most obvious. With virtually unanimous agreement, every major society and world religion condemns indiscriminate sexual activity with multiple partners.

Such activity is seen as being harmful to the relationships between people in society as well as harming the relationship between the creature and his or her creator. To ignore such universal consensus is to ignore something very human and very divine.

However, since "practical" arguments sometimes carry greater weight than the most finely reasoned moral or religious arguments, allow me to offer two practical reasons for abstaining from casual sex.

First, it doesn't produce the happiness it promises. Second, it's stupid. Let's took at those two separately.

Casual sex just doesn't produce the happiness it promises. We hear the argument that "everybody's doing it" (which they are not), but do we ask, "Is anybody happier for having done it?" No doubt such activity may be initially pleasurable and exciting, but I have never seen anyone engaged in indiscriminate sexual activity who impressed me as being very happy.

Among teenagers and young adults, such behavior causes great pain. A genuine survey on the "happiness of life" for sexually active teenagers has, to my knowledge, never been done. However, if it could be done, I would bet that sexually active teenagers would show up as being more likely to drop out of school, to get lower grades, to wind up with lower self-esteem than sexually abstinent students. Just from such anecdotal material as stories of teenage murders (apart from the drug carnage), the incidents consistently center on killing a boyfriend or girlfriend or someone involved with them. When stories of teenage suicides are told, often there are notes or rumors of lost love or rejection in love. The idea that sexual activity produces happiness is a lie.

Second, having sex with multiple partners is stupid. Wilt Chamberlain claims to have had sex with 20,000 women. (I think that Wilt might be confused. He knew that he got two points whenever he scored in basketball, so maybe he multiplied by two when he "scored" elsewhere.)

I don't know how many sexual partners Magic Johnson had before the magic wore off. Several? hundreds? thousands? He should make that clear so if he was stupid he can point out just how stupid it was.

In fact, if I could write the text for Magic Johnson's talks to young people, I would suggest the following: "I want all of you to know how stupid I was. I had the choice to be a hero or a celebrity. I could have been a hero by being as good morally off the court as I was good on the court.

"But I chose to be a celebrity, and I took advantage of it. I took all the money I could get. I took all the women I could get.

"I didn't care about them or about me. I didn't care whether all those women died because of me. I didn't care whether any children that resulted would die. I didn't care whether all those women's other sexual partners died. I didn't care that my wife might die. I didn't care that my own child might die.

"I was stupid. I was selfish. Because I was both stupid and selfish, I'm going to die, and a lot of other people will die. If you're having sex before you get married or having sex with more than one person, you're stupid.

"You've got better things to put your energies into. You can get a good education. You can get a good job. You can make yourself someone that you can be proud of. But if you're having casual sex, you shouldn't be proud of that. You're just plain stupid!"

I think if Magic could give that kind of talk, he would be a real hero!

"Save sex" then involves appealing to the practical and the noble in young people. First, avoid sex because you might get caught, you might die or get one of many sexually transmitted diseases. That's a practical appeal.

Second, avoid casual sex because it's the right thing to do. That's the noble reason. Feelings of sexual pleasure will pass pretty quickly. But the good feelings you get from making something of yourself, the good feeling you get from caring about others, the good feeling you get from having made the world a better place, those feelings last a lifetime.

A Role Model
for Searchers

The hero of much of Eastern and Western literature and culture is the "seeker after truth," the searcher who leaves safe havens to find the Holy Grail, the one who pursues wisdom somewhere else, only to find the treasure where he first began, often within himself. Father Norm Perrin was such a hero.

For those of us who knew Norm as a priest, there is virtually unanimous agreement that he was one of the world's greatest priests – kind, pastoral, sensitive, caring. For those of us who knew Norm Perrin the man, as a human being like ourselves, there were equally fine qualities – seeking, searching, vulnerable, lovable.

Norm found God early in life. It was such early faith that led him to the high school seminary and to ordination as a priest. But in the tradition of the great seekers after truth, Norm continued to search for different ways to serve his God.

He had the courage to move for awhile beyond the secure clerical world of the priesthood to the total insecure secular world. But it was the same Norm. Whether I was scraping paint with him on a bar he renovated or having lunch with him at an ice cream store he ran, he never changed. It was always the same good humor, quick smile and easy laugh.

It was precisely Norm's vulnerability – the way he searched and questioned just like the rest of us – that made Norm so lovable. It was this vulnerable side of Norm that made him seem so much like Jesus in his early life.

Who was this Jesus in his secular occupation as a carpenter? What led him to wander in the desert? What led him to hang around with a wild, hairy person like John the Baptist? Jesus the seeker, the searcher in his private life, the one who spent his whole life searching and just three years in public ministry! Norm Perrin seemed so much like this Jesus.

Like Jesus, who loved Martha and Mary and who found so many women wanting to touch and hug and be with him to help him, so Norm had similar appeal. In his last days of going for chemotherapy, his mother Nancy said that technicians would see him being helped into the clinic by friends and would jokingly say, "Now which woman is it this time?"

Norm's journey took him from owning a bar to being an alcoholism counselor, from state bureaucracies to private enterprise, from one form of helping people to another. But always it was Norm, the servant priest, serving God and serving others in different guises.

Norm ended his life in the same place he had begun it, as a full-time active priest in ministry. Like all the seekers and holy men and women, Norm had to leave home to find home, to make the outward journey that symbolized the inward searching, to seek God out there, only to find God within himself all the time.

Don Quixote is usually remembered as having tilted at windmills. But Don Quixote is forever admired as someone with the courage to go out and to fight for truth and to do what he thought was right. He had the courage to fight the enemy out there even if the real enemy was within himself all the time.

For young people today who seek and question, you could do worse than find a patron saint in Norm. And for young seminarians and young priests, for those who struggle in a confused age and confused society, you might adopt Norm Perrin as your patron.

From his place in heaven I think Norm would say, "Go ahead and make your journey. Go ahead and search and question. But make your journey in faith, and wherever you end up, you'll be where God wants you to be."

MARCH ■

A Lenten Fast That Could Change Your Life

Lent is upon us, and I would like to suggest a penance that could change our lives.

Nostalgically, many of us remember the "good old days" when the church mandated physical fasting during Lent (one full meal a day, with two lesser ones, no food between meals and no meat on Friday). I still encourage people to consider that kind of fasting because although the church does not mandate it, it also does not forbid it.

Yet the fasting I'm going to suggest now is really a fasting from what comes out of our mouths rather than what goes in.

The penance I'm suggesting comes from a quote I saw from a 17th century Spanish mystic, Miguel de Molinos. He said, "Mortify yourself in not judging ill of anybody at any time." Would we dare a penance in which we would not speak ill of anyone for the forty days of Lent?

The reason that I'm suggesting this kind of penance is that it is meant to change our lives. When our emphasis is simply abstaining from food, Lent often becomes an endurance contest. We grit our teeth and endure the season.

Often we can become self-preoccupied, either congratulating ourselves on our success or berating ourselves for our failures. The consolation we have is that we may at least be losing some weight.

Yet Lent is meant not to make us self-preoccupied, but selfless. Nowhere in the Gospels does Jesus indicate a preference for thin people, only a preference for changed people.

The thought of not judging anybody at any time strikes at the heart of much of our lives. How many of us, for example, have spent any time discussing Gary Hart's foreign policy, and how many of us have spent time discussing his personal life?

Which do we find ourselves more interested in, the neighbor who just won a scholarship or the neighbor who was just arrested?

Which gives us greater pleasure, learning of someone else's success or learning of someone else's failure?

One of my fears is that if we did not think ill or speak ill of anyone else, our conversations would turn to dead silence.

Yet would not such silence be revealing? Would we discover that we are mean to others because we do not yet love ourselves? Would we discover that we feel a need to put others down because we really do not believe how much God loves us?

Would we discover that our need to diminish someone else's light comes from a desire to make our own egos shine brighter? How many insecurities and fears and sins would we confront and change if we dared such a penance?

One of the more challenging stories about judging ill of others was told by Dr. Robert Schuller.

He spoke of a young minister who visited a young couple in his church while the husband was dying of cancer. After the husband's death, the minister continued to visit the wife frequently. Neighbors began to notice that when he visited, shades were always drawn in the living room.

Soon the office staff at the church noticed that the minister smelled of perfume when he returned from his visits. Eventually, as rumors grew and gossip spread, the church board demanded the young minister's resignation.

The minister then explained to the board that he continued to visit the widow because during her husband's illness she discovered that she too had cancer. Because of the trauma to her family at her husband's death, she did not want to tell anyone.

Because she was undergoing weekly chemotherapy, she spent much of her time in her bedroom. When she went into the living room to visit with her minister, the bright lights would hurt her eyes so she drew the shades.

In addition, she also developed a strong body odor so she doused herself with perfume to make the visits bearable for the minister.

The minister, of course, was exonerated by this testimony. Yet, would there have been any need for all that pain if others had not chosen to judge him and to speak ill of him?

I'm not sure I'll be able to keep this penance through all of Lent. I'm not so sure that anyone really wants to keep such a penance. Yet Jesus did tell us, "Do not judge, and you will not be judged."

As far as I know, Christianity is the only religion that dares to link God's judgment of us to our judgment of others. Keeping such a penance may not only change us. It may change our eternal destiny.

At the end of Lent, I cannot promise that we will have lost a single pound if we are faithful to this penance. But our hearts will be lighter.

Simply Profound

■

Have you seen the four paintings by Thomas Cole (1801-1848) in the National Gallery of Art or reprinted in books? The four paintings are entitled "The Voyage of Life." Allow me to describe them.

The first painting called "Childhood" shows a little baby in a boat accompanied by a guardian angel setting sail out of a cave (the womb?). The child is headed toward a bright and luscious landscape.

The second painting called "Youth" shows a young man setting out in a boat headed toward a beautiful and lovely horizon (the future?). In the sky is painted a sort of castle, supposedly signifying the dream castles young people build for themselves. This time the angel is on the shore, waving or blessing the youth.

The third painting shows the individual now as an adult. "Manhood" is dark and foreboding. The small boat is being swept along on angry waters, and storm clouds unleash their fury. The man in the boat is gazing heavenward, almost praying. This time, in the midst of the clouds, in one bright spot, the guardian angel is looking down on him. Could this be the storm of life we face in adulthood that often blots out our dreams?

Finally, in the fourth picture we see an old man in the same boat. His guardian angel is right next to him again. The angel is pointing toward heaven as a white space in the clouds appears, and another angel is seen in the clouds pointing the way to heaven.

The artistry is magnificent. The colors are captivating. The message is simple: We come from God and we return to God.

Theologically we could say that it is "old theology," an old picture of life with angels serving as guardians. It was, after all, painted in the early 19th century. However, I like to think of it as "eternally new theology."

It is as "new" as Jesus who spoke of angels watching over us. It is as new as the reality of God's basic promise, "Behold I am with you always." It is as new as the angels who sang when Jesus was a youth. As new as the angels who ministered to Jesus after his temptation and fast of 40 days. It is as new as the angel who ministered to Jesus in the Garden of Gethsemane when he began to sweat blood.

Angels are always representations of the divine in our lives, messengers of God's love from another realm, reminders that God is as much with us as he was with Jesus.

Yes, we are more sophisticated technologically. Yes, we have more refined psychological and sociological jargon. Yes, we have better scientific explanations of things today than we did 100 years ago.

But I'm not sure we have better theological formulations today because I'm not so sure that divinity is any more complicated today.

Jesus always spoke simply of profound matters. He used images of fishing for fishermen. He spoke of planting and fertilizing to farmers. He spoke of everyday life to everyday people.

And Jesus never said life would be easy, but he did promise to stay with us. That's all the paintings said. That's basically all that Jesus said.

The Many Victims of Abortion

■

If I were to write about a plague that has taken more than 21 million lives in the United States since 1973, you might panic and wonder what that plague was. Yet the plague is well known. It goes under the name of abortion.

There are many victims of abortion. The aborted child is only the most obvious.

Next to the child, the person who suffers the most is usually the woman who had the abortion. One such woman wrote, "The sound of the suction machine haunts me to this day. I cannot vacuum a floor without thinking of my abortion."

Olivia Gans, who had an abortion and who founded American Victims of Abortions, writes, "Abortion has many victims. ... There is personal loss because I don't know my child. But the greater loss is that you don't know my child."

In condemning abortion, then, we must be very careful not to condemn women who have had them. They are victims too, and they deserve caring, compassion and forgiveness.

A third victim, often less discussed today, is the man who is partner to an abortion. Drexel University sociologist Arthur Shostak interviewed hundreds of men whose wives or girlfriends had abortions. He says,

"Most of the men ... think about the abortion years after it is over. They feel sad, they feel curious. ... They don't think of it as just an operation. ... They think of it ... as a loss of fatherhood."

With so many victims, why do we, as a nation continue to accept abortions performed at the rate of one every 21 seconds? Basically, we have decided that freedom has greater value than life. Pro-choice advocates have indeed convinced enough people that choosing death for an unborn child is a legitimate freedom. In wrapping the decision in the garb of a "woman's right to choose," personal freedom takes precedence over personal responsibility. Seldom do we hear the question, "Who was responsible for choosing to have sexual intercourse?"

One argument for abortion is that a couple does not want or cannot afford another child. Yet with two million couples on waiting lists for adoption, can anyone seriously say any one baby is not wanted?

Another argument for abortion is in cases of rape. This emotional argument is indeed a challenge. Yet, even victims of the heinous crime of rape have managed to rise above the decision to abort.

Ethel Waters, the gospel singer, was born of rape. Even though she was raised in a slum, she still developed a sense of self-worth and love for God. Her singing brought happiness to millions.

Another anonymous victim of rape tells of scheduling an abortion and then canceling it. She said, "I knew that what I carried inside me was a baby. Now I have a daughter, a beautiful baby girl whom I thank the Lord every day I did not abort."

A third argument for abortion maintains that a fetus is not human life. Yet Dr. Andre Hellegers of Georgetown University Hospital makes short work of that argument, "I do not believe there is any question when biological human life begins. It is at conception. ... To say that it begins at any other time is biological nonsense."

As is often the case, however, logic fails to convince anyone who does not want to be convinced. If the simple statistic of 21 million deaths in 15 years does not convince others that something is seriously wrong, perhaps nothing can convince them. Perhaps the real issue is convincing ourselves.

Cardinal Joseph Bernadin and others have proposed a seamless garment, a consistent pro-life ethic in our approach. What this means is that we not only oppose abortion but also stand firm against the death penalty and nuclear war.

While I like the idea of expanding our notion of pro-life, I find one flaw in this approach. Opposing the death penalty is essentially an effort to spare the life of the guilty. Opposing abortion is essentially an effort to spare the life of the innocent. If we do not give priority to convincing society to spare the innocent, what chance do we really have to convince them to spare the guilty?

One immediately practical thing we can all do to better understand the issue of abortion is to order copies of the "Christopher News Notes" entitled "Life Lines – What You Can Do About Abortion." Many of my quotes and stories were taken from that issue. Copies can be ordered from the Christophers, 12 E. 48th St., New York, NY 10017.

By stuffing these "Christopher News Notes" in our parish bulletins and handing them out at our committee and organizational meetings, we can at least raise our own people's consciousness on this life and death issue.

Until we convince ourselves that life is sacred, we will never be able to convince our world.

Secrets of the
Living Dead

It sounds strange to say it, but wouldn't it be interesting if we treated the living as well as we treat the dead? Have you ever noticed what happens when someone dies?

Suddenly, all is forgiven. The irritating qualities of that person are unimportant. We choose to remember good things about them, not the bad. "Don't speak ill of the dead" is an old saying.

It reminds me of the story of the death of the meanest man in town. At his funeral, the minister asked if anyone wanted to say anything about the deceased. There was a long embarrassed silence as the congregation stared at the floor. Finally, an old farmer stood up and said, "Well, sometimes old Jake weren't as bad as he was most of the time."

In day-to-day living, we often are not that understanding. We often choose to believe the worst about someone else rather than the best. We hold on to grudges as if they were treasures.

Family members sometimes go years without speaking to other relatives. "If you don't have something bad to say, don't say anything at all" usually replaces the correct version of "If you don't have anything good to say, don't say anything at all."

Yet wouldn't life be different if we just realized that everyone we know right now is dying? That happens to be a fact. True, we may not be living under a specific diagnosis of cancer or AIDS or some other illness. But the simple fact remains that life is terminal.

As Evel Knievel said so eloquently, "No one gets out of here alive." Yet rather than being a morbid thought, can it not be a freeing thought?

If we visit a dying person, the last thing on our minds is any intention of harming or making the last days of that person's life more miserable. Rather we are attentive to them. We try to make them comfortable, go out of our way for them.

Suppose we treated every person we met that way? Suppose we decided that helping to make someone else's life easier was not just a good way to help someone die but a good way to help someone live?

Wouldn't a lot of our pettiness and jealously and hard feelings vanish if we gave people during life the understanding we give them at death? Yet the person sitting across the table at us, the driver of the car in front of us – all are dying. Why would we treat that person differently if they have 60 years to live as opposed to 60 days to live?

If we could just believe how tough life is and how short life is for all of us, wouldn't it make more sense for all of us to be kinder to one another?

Lessons From Early Church History

Shortly before Advent, while meditating in the presence of the Blessed Sacrament, two thoughts came that had nothing to do with Advent.

The two thoughts centered on the role of women in the church and the meaning of suffering. To properly develop either thought would require a book, but I have only a few paragraphs here.

The thought about women focused on the Easter scene at the empty tomb. As the women approached the tomb, the angel told them, "Go now and tell his disciples and Peter." Later Jesus would tell his disciples to go and make disciples of all nations. Yet, on Easter morning he told the women to go and make believers of Peter and the disciples.

Many people today have a military model of the church. They see the church as an army with someone on top telling everyone else what to do.

Clearly that was not the model of Jesus. He used the people on the "bottom," namely women, to tell Peter, the first pope, and the rest of the apostles at the "top" what they needed to know. As we learn from the Scriptures, those first women didn't have much luck convincing the first leaders, but at least the women got attention. The leaders took another look at the situation.

Women today who speak for change need to have the same faith and to do the same thing. They also need to believe that the risen Lord who convinced the first leaders to change will convince future leaders as well.

In seeking new roles, women are not competing with men for positions of power but for positions of service.

This leads to my second thought about the meaning of suffering, which is tied to the notion of powerlessness. Elie Wiesel, a survivor of Auschwitz, tells a tragic story, which I have heard before, but repeat here:

The SS hanged two Jewish men and a youth in front of the whole camp. The men died quickly, but the death throes of the youth lasted for half an hour.

"Where is God? Where is he?" someone asked behind me.

As the youth still hung in torment in the noose after a long time, I heard the man call again, "Where is God now?"

And I heard a voice in myself answer, "Where is he? He is here. He is hanging there on the gallows."

Most of us would prefer another answer to the problem of pain and suffering. We would prefer a god who would magically take away pain and suffering.

Instead, we have a God who came to share our pain and suffering. A powerful God would never have needed to come and get dirty and die like humans. Yet a loving God did just that.

Compassion means to suffer with, and we have a compassionate God. The meaning it gives to suffering is that when we suffer, God is most with us.

This does not mean that we seek out suffering. Rather it means that God seeks us out when we suffer. That's why we find God with the powerless rather than the powerful.

So, ultimately, we cannot separate Advent-Christmas from Lent-Easter. We cannot separate the birth of Jesus from his death. We cannot separate the cradle from the cross. In both the message is the same.

The powerlessness of an infant and the powerlessness of the cross let us know that love was the only power Jesus shared because love was the only power he had.

It is only when we love each other and allow ourselves to be loved by each other and by God, that pain is overcome, that defeat turns to victory and death becomes life.

Had Jesus been a god of imperial power, no doubt he would have chosen to be born in imperial Rome. The church, which sometimes exerts imperial power, chose to settle in Rome. Therein lies much of the tension between a powerless God and a powerful church.

As Father Patrick Howell, S.J., so well put it, "The Christian community has never been freed from this tendency towards empire building, imperial enthronements, denial of freedom and the abuse of its very mission to live the life of Jesus for the poor, the mentally ill, the blind, the outcasts of a power-conscious society."

Yet the answer is not found in fighting power with power but by identifying with Jesus, "by sharing our fragility, confident that Jesus has overcome death, that this chaos holds no power over our humanity, that the loving Friend of all the abandoned casts us out of darkness into his own wonderful light."

Craig & Susan, Joseph & Mary

Real-life love stories are the best kind. I've told part of the story of Craig and Susan.

Craig was the handsome high school varsity athlete who developed brain tumors. Susan was the beautiful cheerleader who loved him.

Susan was told by many to forget Craig. Even if he survived the operation for the brain tumors, he might never swallow, talk, walk. He surely would never be able to marry. Susan knew better. "He will walk again. He will walk down the aisle for our wedding."

Through the lonely months of rehabilitation, Craig learned to swallow, talk, walk, and yes, he did walk down the aisle with Susan as his bride!

Where movies and stories end, however, is where this love story continued. Over the course of the next ten years of their marriage, Craig had ten more operations for tumors. Ten more periods of rehabilitation and recovery. Susan stayed with him. Craig had a reason to live.

Next they decided to have a baby! Medical authorities advised against it since Craig's disease that grew brain tumors could be inherited. Family and friends cautioned against it. "How will you support the baby?" "Will Craig be able to help?" "Suppose Craig...?"

Operating on faith and love instead of logic and reasoning, Craig and Susan persisted. Because of the multiple operations and medications, there were difficulties. Finally, miraculously, there was a pregnancy. Then, disastrously, a miscarriage. Distraught but not discouraged, they persisted. Finally, another pregnancy, a lengthy period in bed for Susan and, finally, yes – a baby! Like Abraham and Sarah's, this child of faith and dreams was born against the odds of natural events but not against the odds of God's mercy.

The more I think of Craig and Susan, the more I think of Abraham and Sarah. Abraham lived by faith, not by sight. He began a journey not knowing where he was going, only knowing that God called him. He was promised a child when a child seemed impossible. All Abraham had for guidance was faith. That's all Craig had.

Craig and Susan are more modern, younger versions of Abraham and Sarah. They kept faith when others might have given up. They kept faith in their marriage when others might have broken up.

On the feast of the Annunciation, I thought of Susan when I heard the words of the angel to Mary, "Rejoice, O highly favored daughter! The Lord is with you. Blessed are you among women." I thought of Craig when I thought of the angel's words to St. Joseph, "It is by the Holy Spirit that she had conceived this child."

Abraham and Sarah. Mary and Joseph. Old Testament. New Testament. Craig and Susan – their faith and love a testament to all times, to all loves, to all who kept faith in God.

APRIL

Untitled

The night was dark as Gaius Flavius, centurion, followed the familiar route to the small village outside Jerusalem.

What a miserable three days, he thought to himself, three crucifixions on Friday. Staying on alert on Saturday to see what trouble Barabbas might stir up now that he is loose again. And finally, being asked to post a guard at the tomb of a dead man. What a crazy world this is.

A smile crossed his face as he entered the village. "At least that's all over for now. Now it's time for me to have some fun," he chuckled to himself. "If there is someone else there tonight, I'm going to kick him out right now."

"Hey, Mary," he shouted as he pushed open the door with one hand, with his other hand resting comfortably on his sword, just in case she was not alone. There was no response. Instead he saw Mary alone sitting near a lamp.

"Mary, am I glad to see you!" he said. He unbuckled his sword and laid it to one side as he crossed the room.

As he approached her, Mary just stared into the darkness. From the light on her face he could see that her eyes were bloodshot and swollen. She had obviously been crying. "What's wrong with you?" he asked.

"Jesus is dead," she answered, still not looking at him.

"Jesus who?" he demanded. And then he sighed, "Oh no, not the Jesus we crucified on Friday. Not that crazy prophet from Nazareth."

"He was a good man, Gaius," Mary replied, still not looking at him.

"Of course, he was a good man," snorted Gaius. "Everybody's good when they're dead. Isn't that true?"

He put his hand on her shoulder and she pulled away.

"He was good before he died," she went on. "He was good to children, to the poor, the sick, the elderly. He was even good to me. Can you imagine that, Gaius? Everybody in this village thinks I'm just garbage. But Jesus told me that I was a daughter of God and that my sins were forgiven."

"He was a loser," shouted the centurion. "He appealed to losers and he died a loser's death. But I don't want to lose a night with you."

He reached for her, but this time Mary stood up and pushed him away with a strength that surprised even her.

"Some things have changed, Gaius. I'm not for sale any more. I belong to God."

"This is great," Gaius chuckled sarcastically. "Everything else goes bad. You decide to turn good. This is wonderful. Can I ask what's responsible for this change of heart?"

"Jesus of Nazareth," Mary Magdalen responded calmly. "I looked into his eyes and I felt peace. I heard his voice and I knew joy. He held me and I felt healed. He was a man of wisdom and truth. He was a man of God."

"Wonderful," Gaius mumbled. "I come looking for a comforter, and I find a philosopher."

Then he could control his rage no longer. He roared back. "Do you want to know the God I believe in? I believe in Caesar. He speaks truth. And when he speaks the whole world trembles. He doesn't end up on a cross. He puts other people on crosses. He doesn't need prostitutes and lepers to say nice things about him. The whole world worships him. He is a God of power and wealth and majesty."

Mary smiled at his anger the way a child might pat a lion.

"There would have been a time you might have frightened me, Gaius Flavius. But since I met Jesus, I'm not afraid of anyone or anything."

"Well, you soon will be afraid. It's only a matter of time until we burn your city and destroy your temple. Then we'll see who is stronger, the god of Rome or the God of the Jews."

"You can only burn down so many houses and kill so many people," Mary replied. "But you can't kill love. You can't kill faith. You can't kill a people's dreams. Jesus fulfilled a lot of people's dreams. He was so different. He spoke of forgiveness instead of revenge. Of healing instead of hurting. Of peace instead of war. He gave us a new vision and a new dream."

"Dreams never die," said Gaius. "They just live on in new dreams." He spat the words out contemptuously.

"You just might be right, Gaius Flavius," Mary said as she pulled her cloak around her and gathered up some items.

"Where do you think you're going?" he asked.

"To his tomb. I want to anoint and perfume his body."

"You're going to his tomb," he repeated numbly. Slowly, he walked to Mary and put both hands on her shoulders, this time more gently than before.

"Mary, let me try one last time. You're a beautiful woman. You're an intelligent woman. You know how to survive. Take care of me tonight, and I'll take care of you in the future. A year from now no one will even remember the name of Jesus of Nazareth. Forget about this dead man and believe in a living man."

Mary Magdalen looked at him with eyes that were both compassionate and firm. "I have to believe in Jesus, Gaius, because he taught me to believe in myself. I've been crying over Jesus for two days just trying to understand him. Flesh and blood can't explain the kind of person he was.

"Gaius, he loved everybody. He loved that bunch of phony religious leaders who would not know God if they fell over him. He even loved you Romans who crucified him. He wasn't afraid to love or afraid to speak the truth or afraid to do the right thing, no matter what it cost him. He was good to people and most people are not good to each other. I would rather trust a dead man who was not afraid to die for what be believed than trust a living man who did not believe in anything worth dying for."

She pulled away from Gaius and walked out the door, leaving it standing open behind her.

Stupefied, Gaius called out to her, "When you see him, tell him I'm sorry I thrust that spear in his side. Tell him it was nothing personal. I was just following orders."

Mary did not turn or respond in any way. She just kept walking out of the village toward the tomb beyond the hill.

Gaius didn't follow her. He just stood there staring. His voice had been sarcastic, but his mind was puzzled. He had seen something in her eyes. He had heard something in her voice. He felt something in her presence. He wondered about the power this Jesus had.

He strained to see her now, barely visible in the distance. Overhead the first fingers of dawn were clutching at the sky. A new day was dawning for the world.

Holy Week
Starts at Home

If you want to understand the mysteries of Holy Week, look no farther than your kitchen or dining room table. There the center of family life becomes the symbol of our Christian life.

All of this became so clear to me recently as I sat around the kitchen table with my "adopted" family after a recent funeral. Here was the table where I had shared meals with Sarah and Lionel. Here cards were dealt. Here stories were told and sadnesses lightened.

Fittingly here at the table the rest of the family and friends would gather after the funerals. How conscious I was that some were missing from the circle, and yet, how much I felt their presence. Is that not what Holy Week teaches us?

At the Last Supper, Jesus gathered with his apostles for a final meal and told some final stories and gave a few last words. There he told them that he had to go, but there he told them he would always be found. There where they would most experience his absence would be where they would most experience his presence.

Because they had gathered with the Lord for a meal on Thursday, the apostles were able to cope with the tragedy of Good Friday. It didn't make Good Friday easy. It just made Good Friday bearable.

The apostles still panicked and ran and behaved fearfully, but they knew where to go when the panic was over. They came to realize that Jesus had not promised that life would be easy, but he had promised that he would be with them. So they knew where to go to find him.

Interestingly, when the apostles first heard the news from the women that something had happened Sunday morning, they found only an empty tomb. Geography can only tell us where Jesus is not. Theology tells us where Jesus is. Later that evening, the disciples on the road to Emmaus would meet the living Jesus in the breaking of the bread. They would meet Jesus in a meal.

So as we prepare to celebrate Holy Week, we realize that we are mainly celebrating life. The mystery of Holy Week is telling us to find the sacred in the ordinary. At the kitchen table we meet the Lord.

The first Christians simply did what we do naturally. They gathered in homes to share bread, to tell the stories of Jesus and to love each other. As the young church expanded through its missionary efforts, letters from Saints Peter and Paul and the other apostles began to be read at such gatherings in these "house churches."

As the numbers increased and larger buildings were constructed for worship, the gathering became more formalized but still kept the same structure. Gather the people at the table, the altar. Tell the stories. Break the bread. Go out and love and serve others.

It is in these gatherings together that meaning is found in life. No, life is not easy. Yes, tragedies do happen even to Christians. Belief in God does not protect a believer from tragedy. Belief in God simply protects a believer from despair.

Yet in the gathering as we hear the stories retold and see the bread broken and experience God coming to us in the form of bread and in the form of other people, we realize that we can cope.

So I beg you to try to attend some, if not all, of your Holy Week services at your parish church. Go and experience some of the best liturgies of the year, and then bring home with you the realization that it all started in the home.

The family is a domestic church because it was the family that taught the church before the church taught the family. Every church member was first a family member. Every priest sat at a kitchen table before he stood at an altar.

The church does liturgically what the family does naturally. The reason we have liturgy is to make ourselves aware of God's presence formally so we will not miss his presence in the ordinary.

So try to see your kitchen table as sacred ground. Even scarred, spilled, burned or broken, it is where life is lived and death is mourned. It is where God is found if we only look.

Buying the
Gift of Freedom

■

There's a story told of a little boy walking down the street one day with two wild birds in a cage.

A minister spots the boy and asks him what he is doing. "Not much," the little boy replies. "I caught me some field birds, and I'm going to take them home and play with them."

"What are you going to do with the birds when you tire of playing with them?" asks the minister. "Oh, I'll give them to my cat," the boy replies. "He likes to tear birds apart and play with them too."

The minister pauses and then asks, "How much do you want for the birds?"

"They're not worth much," says the boy. "They're just wild birds."

"How much do you want for them?" the minister asks again.

"Five dollars," says the little boy.

The minister reaches into his wallet, takes out a five dollar bill and hands it to the boy. As soon as the boy is out of sight, the minister opens the cage and sets the birds free.

***

There's a similar story told of a meeting one day between God and the devil.

God asks the devil what he is doing, and the devil replies that he has the world in captivity and has been playing with all the people.

"These human beings are so much fun to play with," the devil says. "They do almost anything I tell them. They wage wars; they rape each other; they murder each other. They mess up their minds with drugs and alcohol. I'm having so much fun playing with them."

"What are you going to do when you're finished playing with them," God asks.

With a scowl straight from hell, the devil replies, "I'm going to damn them forever. I'm going to damn them to eternal misery and suffering."

"How much do you want for them?" God asks gently.

"What are you talking about?" asks the devil.

"I want to set them free," says God. "What price do you want for them?"

"They're not worth anything," says the devil. "If you try to get close to them, they'll spit in your face and kick you around and kill you. Why would you want to save them?"

"I love them," God replies. "What do you want for them?"

"I want the last drop of your sweat and blood," says the devil. "I want your life."

I first heard a version of those two stories on Paul Harvey's radio broadcast on Holy Saturday. Good Friday is the story of Christ paying the price for our redemption. Easter is the story of the happy ending to our story, when God took his life back, when sin and death and Satan were defeated.

The Monday after Easter is celebrated by many as the day when God tricked Satan. Satan is the original April Fool.

***

Since the "20/20" broadcast about a girl's exorcism, no doubt devil possession will get more media attention. Don't lose any sleep worrying about satanic possession.

As one priest put it, "I haven't been afraid of anything since baptism." Stories of possession make good ghost stories but not good Christ stories.

Throughout his public ministry, Jesus battled the devil person by person through his ministry of healing. On the cross, the devil was defeated forever.

So don't waste your time telling scary stories. Tell Easter stories. Christ has set us free from sin and death and Satan. That's good news. That's the Gospel.

Faith for Parents
of the Disabled

■

"I prayed for my son every day for 33 years, and God finally answered my prayers." Those are not the words of St. Monica who prayed so long for the conversion of her son, St. Augustine. Rather, those are the words of a mother of a mentally handicapped son who prayed all that time for a miracle. The miracle was that some day community homes could be built for mentally handicapped people so that, when she and her husband died, her son would have a place to live. Today, through the good work of Catholic Charities, such group homes are a reality, and her son is a happy resident of one of them.

The letter to the Hebrews defined faith as "confident assurance about things we cannot see." So is prayer. Father John Powell once humorously said that many of us have an "over-the-walls" theology of prayer. We throw some prayers over the wall, just in case anybody is there, just in case anybody might be listening. Yet, real prayer, he maintains, is prayer we speak with confident expectation. We need to pray with the expectation that God will answer our prayers and that God's answer will be as good as or better than what we asked for.

Some time ago I heard of someone who said, "Oh, I tried prayer once. It didn't work." Often we fail in prayer when we measure God by our standards and not by his. With God, "one day is as a thousand years.

A thousand years is as a single day." When we don't get the answer we want in the time we want it, we think God didn't hear our prayer. More often we fail to understand a faithful God because we fail to be faithful to God.

I enjoy my annual retreat for the parents of the handicapped on the weekend after Easter partly because I meet such faithful people there. There each year I meet people who not only pray faithfully but who live faithfully. While others may wonder why a child is handicapped, these parents have simply accepted their child. Yes, they share their doubts and worries and fears. Yet, just as courage is not the absence of fear but the overcoming of fear, so too fidelity is not always enjoying the journey but keeping faith in God on the journey.

At the heart of this ministry to the parents of mentally handicapped and to their special people is Sister Justa Walton, IHM. Sister Justa is the Mother Teresa of Baltimore, working with people who often feel forgotten by everyone else. If there is ever a total power failure in Baltimore, there will still be a glow in whatever part of the city Sister is in. These saints just can't turn their halos off.

At the close of the retreat, I shared with these wonderful parents what I imagined the risen Christ would share with them. I would like to share those same thoughts here:

"The time has come to say good-bye. It is not the end. It is just a new beginning on your life's journey. I send you back with some helps for your trip.

"First, I give you peace. It was my first gift to my apostles. It is my first gift to you. Be at peace despite the drudgery, the doubts and the disasters of life.

"Second, I give you hope. Life will be okay. You will be okay. My arrest and torture and death seemed like the end, but you know it was not the end. Tragedy will not have the last word in your life either.

"Third, I give you faith. It is the kind of faith that sustained Fran in 33 years of prayer. It is the kind of faith that has sustained each of you through all the years. I did not bring you this far to leave you now. I will give you faith to sustain you for the rest of the journey.

"Fourth, I give you my presence in your loneliness. Some of you live alone. Others must make decisions alone. Some of you feel alone in your marriages. Just know that you are not alone. I did not promise that life would be easy, but I did promise to stay with you. You cannot change the people in your lives. You can only try to love me living in them.

"Fifth, I give you each other. This exact group may never be together again. Some may return next year. Yet, you have met each other. Don't be afraid to call on each other. Don't forget to pray for each other.

"Sixth, I give you a message from those who have gone before you who are here with me. Your parents, your spouses, your children, your relatives and friends love you as much now as they did then. They send their love, their care, their support, their help. They are your guardian angels. They wait for you even while they assist you.

"Finally, I give you myself. I give you me to be in you. You are my hands and arms and legs. You are my special people who have loved your special people. I give you me because you are so much like me. Thank you for loving so much. Thank you for making me glad that I created the world."

Dear Mr. President: Here's an Idea for Investing in Peace

During this time that we celebrate the death and resurrection of Jesus, an event that profoundly changed our world, I would like to share an idea that I hope can change our world today. The idea I am sharing came to me during a moment of prayer and reflection. I do not think it is too bold to say that the idea came from God.

I communicated the idea in a letter I mailed to the president of the United States. I shared it with him initially in the hopes that he would be able to lend the authority and expertise of his office to making the idea a reality. I now share this with the world.

Please pray with me that this God-given idea bear fruit. The potential for new life for our planet is so enormous that it is truly worthy of being celebrated at Easter.

Here is the letter I sent to the president:

I am writing to share an idea with you because I believe you are in the best position to turn an idea into reality. Before I share the idea, let me briefly introduce myself. I am a Roman Catholic priest of the archdiocese of Baltimore. Currently, I am coordinator of evangelization for the archdiocese. I host a nationally syndicated radio show, "The Country Road." I also do a weekly column in the archdiocesan newspaper *The Catholic Review*. I offer these brief biographical details to assure you that I hold responsible positions, and I am not simply a naive visionary.

My idea, briefly, is to build a sense of human solidarity by creating a means for each individual to share "ownership" of the planet. The idea was sparked by the biblical Jeremiah who bought a piece of property to show symbolically that he owned a piece of the land from which he had been exiled.

Specifically, I am suggesting that working through the United Nations, we encourage each sovereign nation to set aside a tract of land (perhaps a square mile) that could be "sold" in small parcels (perhaps a square inch) to those who would contribute a specified amount to a United Nations' charity (perhaps UNICEF). In other words, every nation in the world would designate a plot of land that could be jointly owned by thousands or millions of people.

What I am suggesting is that the United Nations could issue deeds of ownership so that individuals or groups could literally *own a part of every nation in the world.* The deeds would mean that an individual could own these tiny pieces of property in every country.

My hope for this is that it would build a consciousness among all the peoples of the world of a sense of responsibility for all the people of the world. Suddenly the farthest nation would no longer be a foreign nation. It would now be everyone's country.

In suggesting this I do not mean to "violate" the territorial rights of any sovereign nation. Surely the deeds could be worded in such a way that all owners would forego any attempt to "take possession of" their property in every country.

The idea that I'm putting forth is mainly a symbolic gesture, but it could have a profound impact on how people on this planet view their existence. A sense of responsibility for each other can do away with the possibility of annihilating one another.

There is also an immediate practical side in terms of aiding UNICEF and the children of the world. If the price of each deed were kept low, perhaps $100, I think thousands or millions of people would buy the deed. For some it would just be a novelty, "I own property in every country in the world." Many would buy out of a sense of novelty rather than a sense of solidarity. Yet even then, millions would be raised to help the children of the world.

I am entrusting the idea to you alone because I believe you have the ability to make this a bipartisan issue nationally, and you have the connections through the United Nations to make this a reality throughout the world.

I believe this is a God-given idea. I will put the moral force of my own office behind it. I pray that you will put the considerable force of your office behind it. I would be pleased to discuss this further with you or any of your representatives.

I do not care who gets the credit for the idea. I am open to having the plan altered to fit the realities of political life on our planet. However, I feel committed to the dream of human solidarity in the long run and help for children in the immediate future. The UNICEF idea of saving children can only come to full fruition by creating a world where adults are safe.

Despite the fact that this idea may seem naive in its ideals, please give it serious attention. I can think of no better legacy you could leave to the nation and to the world than helping to bond the human family.

MAY

Thoughts on Mother's Day

I share these thoughts not as my own, but as I would imagine God's Mother writing to us.

My dear children:

First, I hope all mothers feel proud today. Just as I gave birth to God so did you. God lives in every baby. God is where love is, and every baby is filled with love. So thank you for giving birth to God in your sons and daughters, and thanks to all of those who fight for the lives of the unborn and the unloved.

Second, to all the fathers, I would simply say, "Love your wives. The best gift you can give to your children is to love their mother." Children need the love from their parents, but they also need to see the love of parents for each other.

Third, to all of you who are single parents today, please don't feel bad or left out. Remember, I was a single parent too for much of my life. A physical death or the death of a marriage through separation or divorce are all tough. Just remember that God will never leave you and I will never leave you. If a single-parent home was good enough for Jesus, your home will be good enough as well.

Fourth, to all of you who are not physical mothers today, don't think this day is not for you. We give life to people any time we care about other people. If you have helped or loved someone else, you can celebrate the life you have given as well.

Fifth, to all of you who are honoring your living mothers today, remember the best gift you give to Mom is not the present you give today but the time you give to your parents throughout the year. Presents get put away and wear out or grow old. Presents can't replace you. Your mother loves you more than the gift. That's why she likes to have you call or visit.

Remember, your mothers have years behind them that you still have in front of you. So please don't think as Mom grows older that she's just out to make you feel guiltier. As one grandmother put it, "It's just that we know our time is running out, and we want to spend as much of our time with those we love [as we can]."

Remember too the day will come when you'll be glad you made those calls and paid those visits.

Finally, for all of you who are remembering mothers and grandmothers who have died, please remember they are now alive in heaven. And just as all the other saints and angels are aware of what's going on on earth, so are your mothers aware.

Death does not kill a mother's love. Death is just a door, a passage to eternity which makes it possible for mothers to love you with an everlasting love. So as you pray for your mothers and grandmothers, don't forget to pray to them as well. They are the secret saints. They are the quiet saints. They are your personal family saints.

And if you can see the heavens tonight, you will notice a special brightness to night skies on Mother's Day. For today all the mothers shine like stars in that eternal galaxy we call heaven.

With eternal love,
Your Mother Mary

Some Words
for Mom

■

The following is excerpted from Father Breighner's eulogy for his mother:

I want to begin by welcoming all of you and thanking all of you for being here today. I especially want to thank Father Joe Luca, the pastor, and Fathers Kevin Schenning and Dave Smith for all their efforts to make this celebration special here this morning.

I want to thank you too, Your Eminence. My mother always worried about you and asked about you. She set up many a vestment and decorated many an altar for confirmations. She would be both delighted and somewhat embarrassed that someone as important as you attended her funeral.

I express my thanks to all of you in the name of my mother Mary, and in the name of all the children and their spouses – Helen and Mike, Bill and Barb, Margie and myself. I know I speak for the grandchildren and their spouses – Sam and Colleen, Boo and Bruce, Suzanne and her friend Bob. You must know what a support your presence here is to all of us.

Whether your support will be enough to get me through this homily, I don't know. Just in case, I have a relief preacher. You've all heard of relief pitchers. Well, in case I don't make it through, Father Jerry Kenney is going to offer his homily. Jerry is not only one of the finest preachers in the archdiocese but one of the finest priests and human beings in the world.

The readings that we just heard pretty much sum up our feelings today. In the first reading from the second book of Samuel, which my brother Bill read, we heard the story of King David fasting and praying while his son was dying. Yet when his son finally died, he cleaned himself up and had a meal.

Over these past few years during Mother's slow death, we all shed a lot of tears. Unlike David, I'm not so sure our tears are over. In the past we cried for Mother. Now and in the future, we will cry for ourselves. We know Mother is with God. We no longer need to cry for her. Yet we have the emptiness and the void her passing leaves us with. So today, we need not apologize for our tears. They too are God's gifts to us. Our tears help us to draw away the hurt and pain of life.

Behind our tears today however, is not despair but what the second reading from St. Paul's first letter to the Corinthians was all about. Mike Eder did the reading. Mike thinks he is my brother-in-law. I think Mike is my brother. In that reading St. Paul said, "If our hopes in Christ are limited to this life only, we are the most pitiable of men." Yet our hopes today go beyond this life. "Christ is now raised from the dead; ... in Christ all will come to life again."

Faith in God does not protect a believer from tragedy. Faith in God only protects a believer from despair. Today, our hearts are heavy with loss, but our spirits are light with hope.

The first two readings, then, sum up our feelings. The Gospel reading from Luke I believe sums up Mom's life. In today's Gospel we saw Anna, the lady who lived in the temple, who took Jesus in her arms. Today we bury Mary, the lady who lived in Our Lady of Mt. Carmel Church, whom Jesus has taken in his arms. Father Hank Milkowski mentioned a few months ago that someone had commented, "Every time the church doors were open, Mary Breighner was there."

Those words were true. Mother had various addresses in this area during her life. At one time she lived in a small house in Essex, later a small apartment in Hawthorne. Then there were those many years in an apartment in Mars Estates – now known as the Village of Tall Trees. (Frankly, I miss Mars Estates. In school I used to say that I went the longest distance to school. I had to come all the way from Mars). Mom's final apartment was at Hopkins Village. Those were the places she took her meals and her mail. But here at Mt. Carmel is where she really was at home. It's good that we have a chance to have a home Mass together for Mom.

Here was the place her voice could be heard singing at evening devotions to Mary and at benediction. Here her music could be heard when she played the organ at Sunday Mass. Here she carried away thousands and thousands of albs and other vestments to be washed and pressed. (Every time I went to take a shower at home, there was always an alb hanging on the curtain rod.) Here Mom worried about altar linens and altar decorations.

Here were her things, and here were her activities. Here were the people she loved like a family. Here were the priests she always loved and, I suspect, at times drove crazy. Here were the sisters and religious she idealized and idolized. Here in past years was the Sodality. And here for so many years was her beloved Altar Society. Many years ago saintly Monsignor Kerr asked Mom to form an altar society. Here were the people she loved right after her own family. Here were Margaret and Millie and Helen and Virginia and Marie and Charlie and Betty and Donna and Kathleen and Catharine and on and on and on in a litany of the saints as long as life itself.

My mother died with so few possessions that it would break the heart of the worst scrooge. My mom spent her life giving herself away instead of storing things up. Even in death she gave away her eyes. Yet my mother died with a treasure that many a king or emperor or pharaoh would have envied. She died with a wealth of friends. She died in the friendship of people who had known her most of her life or for only a few years or weeks or days.

Here in her home at Mt. Carmel her friends sustained her through life until that time when the hospice personnel at Stella Maris would be as angels of mercy, escorting her to the very gate of paradise.

At the heart of all of her other friendships, though, was one special, quiet and steady friendship. That was her friendship with God. Here at daily Mass and in her daily rosary, here in her novenas and devotions, here God became a friend. God's presence in her life sustained her life through tragedies and heartbreaks and disappointments so great we wondered how she bore them. His presence in her life was so powerful, though, that Mom's sweet smile, her pleasant manner, her genuine spirit, her genuine care for others and her constant sense of humor would lead those who knew her only slightly to never guess the terrible burden she had carried through life.

Perhaps, the one line that most summed up her positive attitude toward life was the expression, "Some people are too great to be famous." She had been recognized by God, and she neither wanted nor sought any other recognition.

Sandy Fink, her friend and social worker from Stella Maris hospice, had given her a book, a diary to record her thoughts over these final months. Mom had not written a single word. But there was one final poem taped to her refrigerator door. (I guess she figured if she put it in her Bible I'd never find it, but putting it on the refrigerator made it a sure bet for me.)

Mom often let other writers speak her feelings. Just as she was famous for birthday and Christmas cards and cards for all occasions – she would spend hours searching for just the right words and would then underline certain phrases in the cards – so too I think this tiny poem by Florence Holbrook on her refrigerator inspired her and was a reflection of the life she lived. It is simply entitled: A Prayer

Not more of light, I ask, O God
But eyes to see what is;
Not sweeter songs, but power to hear
The Present melodies.

Not greater strength, but how to use
The power that I possess;
Not more of love, but skill to turn
A frown to a caress.

Not more of joy, but power to feel
Its kindling presence near;
To give to others all I have
Of courage and of cheer.

Give me all fears to dominate
All holy joys to know;
To be the friend I wish to be,
To speak the truth I know.

A poet wrote those words, but Mom lived them.

So, last Thursday, the friend that Mom knew through life came to take her home. Just as Simon looked at Jesus in today's Gospel and knew it was okay to go, "Now, Lord, you may dismiss your servant in peace according to your word," when Mom saw the face of Jesus last week, she knew it was all right to go also. She had wanted to live to see her great-grandchild, and I think God promised her that she would see the child in a way more beautifully that she had ever dreamed. This was not the God who takes away life but rather the God who restores life after death has tried to take it away.

So, Mary, named after the mother of Jesus, now lives with Jesus and his mother. Mom, whose favorite color was orchid, now blends eternally with Mary, whose favorite color is deepest blue.

And tonight, as you go out into the night, you will not see darkness and stars, but you will see a mantle of deepest blue, sparkling with a mother's care. And, tonight, as you look into the heavens you will see one more star of love woven into the fabric of heaven. And there in the midst of the night – there shines an eternal day.

Upset? Just Put It
In Perspective

The following letter was sent home by a girl in college:

Dear Mom and Dad:

The dormitory I'm living in burned down last night. Unfortunately, the fire started in my room where my roommate and I were smoking pot. Fortunately, my boyfriend said I could move in with him. We were going to get married anyway before the baby was born. Although he doesn't have a job and has never worked, I still love him so. He said we could live with his father who has a room above his gas station in Anchorage, Alaska.

> *Love,*
> *Your daughter, Cindy*

P.S. None of the above is true. The dormitory did not burn down. I do not smoke pot. I am not pregnant. I am not moving in with my boyfriend. I am not going to Anchorage, Alaska. I did flunk chemistry. I just wanted to put that in perspective.

Perspective is something we all need. In a stress management workshop recently, the speaker suggested that life is not just what happens to us. In other words, we can make things worse than they are.

A flunked subject is no more the end of the world than that scratch on our new car. Not making the team is no more a cause for suicide than not getting that new job or promotion.

At the time, something can seem much worse than it is. A nice gift to ourselves is to put whatever happens to us in perspective. As a wise person once observed, "Do we ever pause to thank God for what did not happen to us?"

For Christians, faith gives us ultimate perspective on all the events of life. Death is a terrible thing but not quite as terrible when we realize that there is a loving God there to meet us on the other side of death, a God who promises the living that they will meet "lost" loved ones again.

A serious illness or accident can be an awful thing, but it becomes a little less awful when we believe that God will stay with us and help us to endure the pain and to continue living with whatever limitations we may have to bear.

In saying all of this, I do not mean to imply that getting perspective is always easy but simply to say that perspective is always possible. This does not mean that we cheat ourselves out of our feelings of loss and anger and depression.

Christianity does not mean that we cease to be human. Christianity is about transforming our humanity.

I do not for a second believe that Jesus' faith made the pain of the cross any less real. However, faith in a Father who would transform death and defeat into life and victory made it possible for Jesus to suffer with hope while the man hanging next to him could only wallow in despair.

Life is not easy. Nothing we can say or do will ever make it easy. However, life is better than we sometimes think it is because God has entered human history and because he has a special interest in and love for each one of us.

It is that belief that gives us perspective when we experience those dark nights of the soul.

Mary, Star of Evangelization

The story is told of a little boy praying for a new bike for Christmas. He began by praying, "Dear Jesus, if you give me a new bike, I'll be good for a week."

He thought about it for a minute and then prayed, "Dear Jesus, if you give me a new bike, I'll be good for a day."

Realizing that even a day was a long time, the little boy looked over into the manger scene, took the Blessed Mother out of the set and hid her in his desk. He then prayed, "Dear Jesus, if you ever want to see your mother again..."

Mothers play an important role in all our lives. As the mother of Jesus and the mother of the church, Mary has always played an important role in the lives of Christians.

As we begin a Marian Year, a time of special devotion to Mary, is it not a good time to honor Mary under another title: Mary, Star of Evangelization?

Mary, in essence, was the first evangelist, the first to share the good news of Jesus with the world. Specifically, there were three things that Mary did that distinguished her in that role.

First, Mary was open to the Word of God. She both heard the words of the angel and invited God's spirit into her life. She allowed God to take on her flesh, to become real in her life.

Second, Mary gave birth to Jesus into the world. She did not keep Jesus to herself as her personal Lord and Savior.

Third, she shared Jesus with the rest of the world. She recognized that God was not just my God but also our God. We who love Mary must move from admiration to imitation. We cannot stop with devotions to Mary but must make that important step of leading ourselves and others to adoration of her son.

How do we become evangelists in imitation of Mary the evangelist?

Essentially, we follow the same three steps.

First, we must allow God's Word into our lives. We must make the effort to open the pages of Scripture, now available in so many translations, and to become a part of Bible study groups, so numerous in our parishes. We must allow the words of God to become the Word of our lives.

We need to become comfortable with just being silent in the presence of God and allowing him to speak to us. Unlike Mary, are we not sometimes so busy that if God called us, he would get a busy signal?

Second, we must give birth to God in our lives. God chose to take on flesh in Mary because he always chooses to take on flesh. God does indeed live in the world in creation, in the sacraments, in the Eucharist, but he always wants to live in us. Are we aware of how special we are to God that he wants to make his home in us?

Thinking of God's home, I recall a true story of a little boy who took his lunch into church one afternoon. The other children ran to tell Sister that Johnny was eating in the church.

Sister quietly walked up behind the little boy and saw how happy he was. She knelt behind him and asked, "Do you think this is an appropriate place to eat?"

"Oh yes, Sister," the little boy replied, "it's my Father's house, isn't it?" Are we as aware that God wants to make us his temple, to share his life with us?

Third, if we would imitate Mary, we too must share Christ with the world.

Too often, I fear, we take a sort of baby-sitting mentality with Christ. Just as a couple leaves the child home with a sitter, we too so often leave Christ at home.

Yet it is the marketplace that so desperately needs God's presence.

All studies indicate that people join a church or return to church largely because of the influence of a relative, neighbor or friend.

Let us pray to Mary this year especially for those who have no church. Let us pray to Mary that she will inspire us to imitate her in the work of evangelization. Let us make this our daily prayer for the Marian Year:

O Mary, as a star once led people long ago to your son, may you be the star of evangelization to continue to lead others to Jesus today.

You were the first evangelist. You were open to welcome God's Word into your life. You gave birth to Jesus into the world. You shared him with everyone.

Help us to welcome God as he comes to us in the Scriptures and Eucharist. Help us to give birth to him in our lives. Help us to be bold in sharing him with others by words, actions and the witness of our lives.

O Mary, inspire us to inspire others to meet our Lord, Jesus Christ, who lives with the Father and Holy Spirit, one God, forever and ever. Amen.

JUNE ▪

The Marvels of Marriage: 10 Ways to Make It Work

As an unwed father living in a home of unwed fathers (a rectory), what would I know about marriage?

Even though I have lived life as a single person, I have prepared a few couples for marriage and, sad to say, seen more than my share of unhappy couples in my counseling practice.

What advice would I give to young people preparing for a life together? Let me suggest 10 things:

First, enjoy marriage! Isn't it interesting how so much advice starts with bad stuff? No wonder most young people don't want to listen to us "old" folks. We always seem to emphasize what might go wrong. Yet, I believe a happy marriage is one of God's best gifts to us.

God said at the very beginning of the Bible that it is not good for man to be alone. It isn't. If you have found that special someone, enjoy that special someone.

Second, don't be afraid to trust. The key to love is trust. A healthy marriage involves a commitment so complete that one can be totally open, totally honest, totally giving to that other person. Remember, marriage is unlike any other relationship on earth. We may not want to make ourselves that vulnerable to anyone else.

Yet in marriage, as soon as I start holding back, as soon as I "can't say that because he'll get mad," as soon as I start making excuses for not being honest, then I start to undermine the relationship. Marriage is for emotionally healthy people.

Third, don't be afraid to ask for help. If you sense that "something is wrong," it probably is. Getting counseling before marriage is one of the best investments you'll ever make in preventive medicine. Once you are married and things are going bad, don't put off getting help. Too often couples will say, "But I can't afford counseling." Counseling is cheaper than divorce. Divorced people pay financially the rest of their lives.

Fourth, don't go into a marriage expecting that you will change your spouse. One of the biggest mistakes couples make is expecting that they will be able to rearrange their partner. You can't. If you see character-istics in your intended spouse that irritate you, better to talk about them before you get married. Real love is accepting someone else the way he or she is. That's tough, but that's what love is all about.

Obviously, I am not talking about abusive or destructive behavior. That has to be confronted and stopped, or the marriage will not survive.

Fifth, while you will not be able to change your spouse, do not be surprised that your spouse will change in ways you might not expect or like. The person we marry is not always the person we are married to. I can't tell you how many times I have heard something like, "He was just so sweet and wonderful before we married, and now he's mean and puts me down and yells at the children."

Intimacy can bring out the best in us, and it can bring out the worst in us. In day-to-day living, aspects of his or her personality that you never knew about will surface. Children, too, change a relationship forever. Never have children to help the marriage. Get help to make your marriage better and then have children.

Sixth, make a genuine effort to develop a personal spiritual life, and make an effort to share your faith life. This is actually the most important thing you can do for your marriage, but I figured if I started this list talking about God, you would think this was preachy and you wouldn't read any more of it.

So I put God here in the middle. That's where God belongs – in the middle of your marriage. The old advice is true: make God the third party in your marriage.

Data indicate that Catholics have lower divorce rates than other believers. Apparently, a strong appreciation for the permanence of marriage, a commitment to family, a waiting period before weddings are performed and marriage preparation courses have an effect.

There is further data indicating that people of all faiths have lower divorce rates than people of no faith. God makes a difference. A faith community makes a difference.

Seventh, early life experience has a dramatic influence on our adult life. This is especially true in marriage. Children of divorced parents tend to have a higher divorce rate themselves. Children of alcoholics often marry alcoholics. Abused children tend to abuse their children.

We may hear people say, "I'm not going to be like my mother." "I'll never marry anyone like my father." Yet, very often we do end up a great deal like our parent of the same sex, and we often marry someone remarkably similar to our parent of the opposite sex.

I knew a lady who would say to men courting her daughters, "Take a good look at me, and you'll see what your wife will look like one day." She was not far from the truth.

Eighth, the best thing you can do to make your marriage happy is to make yourself happy. In other words, people who are unhappy and depressed before marriage sometimes have unrealistic expectations that marriage will make everything wonderful. It won't. Sometimes the disillusionment lies heavy on a marriage.

Expecting someone else to make you happy is unfair to yourself and to your partner. The more at peace you are with yourself, the happier you are personally, the more "together" you are, the more you will bring to your marriage. Love is wanting to give our best to someone else, not just wanting to get from someone.

Ninth, we do not fall in love for purely logical reasons. Romance involves hearts and flowers and feelings. Thank God for them, and enjoy them. However, while we may be attracted to someone on a feeling level, there are also some hard, cold, logical reasons why people stay together. Let me give a few examples.

First, the higher the income, the lower the divorce rate. Yes, the tabloids talk about the divorces of the rich and famous. Money doesn't guarantee success. However, research indicates that the single issue most couples fight about is money. The lack of money is one of the biggest strains on a marriage.

Second, the higher the educational level, the lower the divorce rate. Greater education not only usually guarantees greater income, but it also provides us with greater insight into the complexities of life. School may seem like a pain in the neck when you are young, but it can be one of your best investments in yourself and in your marriage.

Third, couples who marry later have a higher success rate than those who marry at a younger age. There is no substitute for life experience, and maturity sometimes takes time.

Tenth, keep faith in each other. Hundreds of millions of couples throughout history have had successful marriages. You can too. We live in a throwaway culture. Don't throw your partner away when times are tough. We live in a culture that demands instant pleasure. Marriage is not always pleasurable.

Love often really begins when some of the feelings begin to wear off. After all, it's easy to love someone when all is well. It's tough to love when times are tough, but that's what real love is.

These are just ten quick thoughts about getting married. Probably I could have listed a hundred. Hundreds of books already have been written with countless ideas. Read them and learn more.

In the Bible, there is a passage from one of St. Paul's letters to the people who lived in Corinth. These words are frequently read at wedding ceremonies but not always lived in marriages. Allow me to quote them:

"Love is always patient and kind; it is never jealous. Love is never boastful or conceited; it is never rude or selfish; it does not take offense and is not resentful. Love takes no pleasure in other people's sins but delights in the truth. It is always ready to excuse, to trust, to hope and to endure whatever comes. Love does not come to an end."

Three Cheers for all the Volunteer Religious Educators

■

They are God's quiet army.

They are present in literally every parish.

They are gentle heralds of God's good news.

They are the thousands of volunteer religious educators who teach in our parish programs.

As the school year winds down, we need to take a moment to thank the people who teach our children about God. In many ways they may be the most important people in our children's lives. The impression they make and the image of God they give can last a lifetime.

Most often I think religious educators undervalue themselves. Like the rest of us in ministry, they often wonder what difference they have made. "I did my best. I hope the children got something out of it" is how some look at their efforts.

Yet in my work in evangelization, I can say that no effort for our children is wasted.

One of my saddest experiences in working with adults is to meet people who have had no religious education. When I say no education, I mean none. They do not know how to make the sign of the Cross. They have no knowledge of the Bible, the sacraments, the Eucharist, or even why there is a church or whether God really matters.

In our age of broken homes and broken families, I fear this number may be increasing. Under the pressures of survival, sending their children to religion class often takes the lowest place in some parents' priorities.

Still, against the odds, our religion teachers go on. They go on preparing our young people for the sacraments. They go on finding creative ways to make the Bible stories come alive. They go on even when the kids don't seem to care and their parents show no appreciation. They go on because Christ asked them to go on and they take Christ seriously.

We can't begin to estimate the time and energy so many of our teachers give. Some open their homes and have classes right in the neighborhoods. Others spend countless hours creating the right atmosphere in classrooms: making banners, shopping for religious symbols, baking cookies for class celebrations, all wrapped around the nitty gritty of lesson plans and workbooks.

While giving a parish mission, I met one teacher who regularly acts out scenes from the Scriptures with her class. One week she built a boat and had the children experience Noah's Ark or had them feel what it was like to be with the apostles and Jesus on the lake.

At other times she had them experience the Last Supper or the sower in the field or any of a host of the parables of Jesus. When I asked her if she told others about her work, she quietly responded that she did not want any attention.

In contrast to the zeal of these volunteer teachers is the apathy or near hostility of some parents. Far from lavishing praise on these dedicated people, some parents act as if the effort of sending children to class is an unbearable burden. Parents who would not think of having their children miss ballet or soccer practice often treat religious education as an optional activity.

Too often we hear the old line, "I'm not going to raise my children in any faith. I'm going to let them decide as adults."

Unfortunately, no religious education is precisely an education in the unimportance of religion. Children who grow up without any faith experience simply conclude that faith is not a very important experience. The way to educate for religious freedom is precisely to raise our children in a faith so that as adults they have something to make a decision about.

Yet, despite all the limitations and resistance, our religion teachers still go on. They are indeed an army of faith who come not to conquer but to serve. Behind them, serving them, are parish DREs, AREs and CREs; and behind them, serving everyone, is the Division of Religious Education, one of the hardest working divisions in the archdiocese.

From my perspective, I like to think of these people as the church's first evangelists. They are sowing the first seeds of faith in children who may not be all that excited about religion and sowing seeds for parents who may not be all that involved in religion.

Yet, just as grace builds on nature so too an adult faith must be built on a childhood faith. The better the foundation, the better the chance for growth.

Even when that growth does not follow the path we would like, it remains forever true that it is much lot easier to invite back to church an "inactive" Catholic than to invite back to church an "unchurched" person who has never had any religious training.

Success &
the Skipjacks

■

Perhaps you saw the fun page ad in *The Catholic Review* of May 29. It was a list of all the eighth grade graduates who had won scholarships to a Catholic high school. One particular name – Christopher Kristofco – caught my attention. He is not only a scholar but an athlete and all-around great human being.

We wonder sometimes what goes into the making of an excellent human being. What gives an individual that cutting edge to achieve? Great parents and family? Certainly. An excellent Catholic parochial school, such as Immaculate Heart of Mary? Yes. A deep faith in God that is nourished by family and friends? Of course.

But is there another influence, often overlooked by sociologists and psychologists and other behavioral scientists?

Yes. Hockey!

Hockey? You see when Christopher was only a child in arms, his father would take him to the Civic Center (now The Arena) to watch the local hockey team. When Christopher reached the age of reason, about age 7, with full consent of his will and sufficient reflection, he continued to choose to go to hockey games with his father.

How did this help him? In ways too numerous to mention. First, it sharpened Christopher's math skills. "Dad, how many minutes did

Schludelberg get in the penalty box?"

Second, it honed his vocabulary and foreign language skills. "Dad, what does 'icing the puck' mean?"

Third, it gave him an arena for observing the complexity of human relations skills. "Dad, why did Kurdle break his hockey stick over Lemieux's head?"

Fourth, it improved his "hand-eye" coordination as he participated in puck shooting contests between periods. But, enough! You know what I mean.

The fine line between "excellent" and "very excellent" is the hockey advantage. I share all this because Christopher has two younger sisters, Colleen and Caitlin, and a younger brother, Kevin. They also have been to hockey games. If you want to level the playing field in competing with them for future scholarships, I beg you to get your kids to a hockey game as soon as possible.

So I salute all those young people who won scholarships. I salute their parents who sacrificed to send them to parochial schools. I salute their teachers and administrators who sacrificed personally and financially to keep parochial and Catholic high schools open. I salute all those who may never have won a public award but who have won the highest award of all – the values that a Catholic education gives to young people. I salute Christopher Kristofco.

And for Christopher, my mind goes to a distant day in the future when a large crowd will gather at some testimonial dinner in his honor. At that time in life he will be a captain of industry or a noted neurosurgeon or a leader of some social program or a teacher or an athlete or a priest. At the end of the meal he will rise to the applause of the assembled multitude, and he will lift a glass as a toast.

He will say something like, "I owe my success in life to my loving parents and family. I owe my success to my excellent educational foundation at Immaculate Heart of Mary parochial school. I owe my success to my advanced education at Calvert Hall College High School. I owe my success to all of you who have stood by me through the years."

Then his voice will crack a little, and as he begins to fill up, he will speak over his choked up emotions, "But most of all I owe it to the Skipjacks!"

Skipjacks, for all you do, this scholarship's for you.

Living the Call
to Faithfulness

I recall a retreat master once speaking about the "silent holy ones," the people who sustain others by their quiet prayers. My Aunt Kathryn, Sister Wilma Breighner, fits that description.

Sister Wilma celebrated her 50th anniversary recently as an Ursuline nun. She's the youngster in religious life in her immediate family. Her two sisters, Sister Theodora and Sister Helen, are celebrating 58 and 61 years respectively in the Ursuline Order as well.

In referring to my aunt as a silent holy one, I do not mean to overlook her active ministry as a speech therapist. Nuns like my Aunt Helen have a way of doing as much in retirement as others do in full-time work.

What I'm referring to is really the contemplative attitude my aunt brings to her life and her work. Her quiet nature predisposes her to being at ease in the presence of God. Sister Wilma reminds us that what we do takes on infinite value when we do it for God.

Personally, I believe that I might not even be a priest if it were not for the praying power of my aunts. Their prayers have sustained me at times when I'm sure I was not even aware they were sustaining me. I have this fantasy that whenever the pope considers firing me, he looks at my aunts and says, "Well, at least they're holy. Three out of four's not bad."

Whenever I visit my aunts and visit with so many of the other active sisters and retired sisters at their motherhouse in Louisville, Ky., I go away with a sense of profound respect for all religious women.

Here are the women who have left all for the Lord. They have given up, not just the family of origin, but also the possibility of families of their own. Here are women who live real poverty. While the aged and infirm have air conditioning in Marian House, the rest sweat out the summer heat with only a few fans. Here are people who have dared to live lives of gospel simplicity.

Sadly, the world often does not notice their sacrifice or their witness. The week that I was in Louisville for the jubilarians' celebration, the big event in town was the Home and Garden Show. Virtually every hotel was packed with people for this event.

While I do not want to demean people's interest in homes or gardens, I do wonder what the world would be like if they spent an equivalent amount of time tending to their spiritual lives.

Would we spend more time in prayer if we really believed we were temples, homes of God's Spirit? Would we plant virtues in our lives with the energy we spend planting seeds in our gardens? Would we water with love our actions toward others with the same energy we water our lawns? Would we tend to broken relationships with the same energy we tend to house repairs?

Religious orders remind us of religious priorities.

It's no secret that religious orders are struggling. Vocations to the religious life are down. There are those who believe we are at a turning point in history. There are those who believe that many of the orders and structures that we grew up with will not endure much longer in the church.

Yet, I think the real test of religious faith is being faithful without knowing what the future will be. We do not try to tell God how to run the future. We simply try to be faithful to what we know now.

A vocation is not in the genes. A vocation is only in Jesus. What will survive every structure will be individuals who dare to listen to the call of Jesus and who follow him as best they can.

Lay people, married and single, are doing and will continue to do many of the things that only priests and religious once did. We are not just graciously burying the past, but we are planting for the future. Transformation, not destruction, is always the mark of God.

A wise person once said something to the effect that "Now is the only time we have to live. All else is memory or hope."

We need grateful memories, memories grateful to religious orders, such as the Ursulines, who have preserved and are preserving Christianity through another religious Dark Ages.

And we need hope, hope that a gracious God, who got us this far, will not leave us now.

For the present, we try to follow the words of Mother Teresa, "We are not called to be successful. We are called to be faithful." Nothing may turn out the way we think it will. But everything will turn out the way God wants it to.

So You Think
You Have Problems

■

So you think you have problems? Well, let me tell you.

The other day I read something that makes our lives look like picnics. For the first time in my life I read the *Baltimore Sun* column by Lynda Hirsch which offers a brief synopsis of each soap opera.

Let me confess that I have never watched any soap opera in its entirety. I had never even read a synopsis of one.

Now, however, I know why they're so popular. The "soaps" depict people whose lives are even worse than ours. The old saying that "misery loves company" is only partially true. What misery really loves is someone else more miserable.

Allow me to quote just one capsule summary of one soap opera. I will not name the soap for fear I may be accused of giving free advertisement. The summary reads:

"Holden is speechless when Angel arrives at the AIDS ball on Henry's arm and later asks her for a divorce, claiming he is still in love with Lily. Susan admits to Emily she can't get over feelings for Bob. Bob and Kim are about to make love when she pulls back. Lien informs Duke she is ready to make love to him. Angry that Lucinda wrote an article on Philip Lombard, Ellie quits her job and considers working for Montgomery Associates. Joe and Lyla hear Casey's final plea that Margo disconnect his life support on a cassette recording. A growth on Bob's face concerns Kim and Susan."

See, and you thought you had problems. As I read that account, I think there are at least four of the Ten Commandments violated and five of the Seven Deadly Sins committed! I've had my bad days, and you probably have too, but I don't think we're close to that record.

To be fair, there were some acts of virtue mentioned. Attendance at an AIDS ball seems to indicate some compassion for suffering people. Kim's "about to make love when she pulls back" seems to indicate temptation being overcome. And Kim and Susan worrying about that growth on Bob's face shows some kindness.

See, just as the devil can quote scripture, so even soap operas have some redeeming qualities.

Why am I writing about soap operas? Somehow or other they help to put other problems in perspective. Good people seem to watch them without harmful side effects. Good Catholic mothers and grandmothers watch them, and they don't feel the least inclined to imitate them.

Does this mean I'm endorsing them? No, I haven't watched any. But I do think it serves to remind us that while the media may be influential, people with good values are able to resist bad values.

Therein may lie the moral of this story. I want to congratulate all the priests and religious and lay people who have helped to pass Christian values on to others. People who have the truth are able to see through falsehood.

To misquote a famous quote, "The best defense is a good defense." In other words, if we want to prepare another generation to live the values of Christ, then give those values to them.

Get involved in your parish's youth and educational programs. If our young people are told the truth about God, they won't fall for the lies of the world.

In closing, I would like to offer a prayer I composed using exclusively the titles of soap operas. I have heard similar prayers, but I could not find any copies so I wrote my own. I hope you find it helpful.

O God, "As the World Turns," help us to remember that you have said, you are "All My Children." As your children, we ask you to be our "Guiding Light" whether we live in "Santa Barbara" or spend time in a "General Hospital." Since we have only "One Life to Live," may we realize that life does not belong to "The Bold and the Beautiful" or "The Days of Our Lives." Bless us through all "Generations" and lead us to "Another World" with you. Amen.

The Sun, the Sand, the Symbols

A trip to the beach. Maybe there's more to it than meets the eye.

First, of course, there's the water. During the war with Iraq, a chaplain friend said he might be called to Saudi Arabia. I replied, "Nice beach. Not much water." Water is the heart of going to the beach. It's the life and purpose of the trip. Our sacramental life begins in the waters of baptism. We are born again with a new purpose and new heart.

Second, we oil ourselves up on the beach with suntan lotions and sun blockers. In baptism, for confirmation and during the anointing of the sick, we oil ourselves up to prepare for the journey, for strength on the journey and for the last journey home. We try to block out evil or at least lessen its influence.

Third, most folks first go to the beach as families. The sacrament of matrimony prepares people to be parents. Life's too long to walk alone but just long enough if we walk together.

Fourth, at the beach someone has to prepare food. The sacrament of holy orders ordains certain individuals to prepare the Eucharist, to break bread to feed the family. It was along the shore, breaking bread, that the apostles conversed with the risen Lord.

Fifth, we need something to read between plungings into the water. The Bible becomes good reading material near the sea – lots of stories about dividing the waters, walking on water and drinking water.

Sixth, we pack extras to make life better at the ocean. We always take the theological virtues of faith, hope and charity. Faith that the journey will be safe. Hope that it won't rain, that the day will be good. Charity toward others when we get there. We want for others the same good time we want for ourselves.

Seventh, there will be nicks, cuts, abrasions and broken bones on occasion. We take the sacrament of penance, of confession, along in life to keep patching up our poor decisions.

Eighth, we take the cardinal virtues with us in our bags. Prudence in knowing when to come out of the sun. Temperance in not eating or drinking too much. Fortitude in having the courage to do the right thing even when it's not easy. Justice in wanting to share what we have to help others have as good a time as we are having.

Ninth, we need the lifeguard. Is not the lifeguard always a symbol of Jesus? We need someone to save us when we can't save ourselves, someone to alert us when we're in too deep, someone to watch over us when we just want to forget for awhile. We need someone like us, someone who cares about us, someone willing to risk getting hurt to save us. Don't we all need a lifeguard to help each of us to be lifeguards to each other?

Finally, don't we all need a crowd on the beach? Okay, maybe we all don't like too large a crowd, but isn't it more fun to watch others enjoy themselves, to hear children squeal, to know others are like us? Isn't that what the church is meant to be God's support group? A group of people who become community and family to each other.

In the course of a week at the ocean, we find ourselves spreading our blankets next to the same people, looking for that familiar face, meeting new friends. The church is that group of people on the sands of time who group together on the shore of eternity. Here we laugh together, play together, mourn together, celebrate together, grow up together and eventually, die together.

Here we discover the presence of God in each other and in ourselves. Here our hearts yearn together for the fullness of the revelation of God when God and his people are one together. Here on life's shore, we yearn for the land of eternal sunrise, where "the sun will not harm you by day, nor the moon by night."

A trip to the beach? Maybe it's more than it seems.

God Should Be
as Exciting as
a Baseball Game

How did we ever make God boring? For most of my life I have been a sports fan. I've seen people spend weeks looking forward to a game. I have seen thousands of people packed in a stadium shouting, clapping, stomping and generally going wild. Yet, when I hear many people talk of going to church I hear that time-worn expression, "I don't go to church. It's too boring."

How did we ever make God boring?

To ask that question is not to be irreverent. I realize that worship is not meant to be strictly an emotional experience. I personally like quiet and silence. I even liked the Latin Mass.

My point here is not to talk about styles of worship but to talk about our attitude toward God. Is God not worth getting excited about, at least once or twice in life?

The problem is not that people do not believe in God. The problem, I fear, is that people who do believe in God do not act as if they believed.

To say that is not to endorse any particular style of worship as being better than others, nor is it to say that we Christians should go around with perpetual smiles or feelings of ecstasy all of the time. Life does not always feel good, nor can it always be good.

Yet is it not a sad commentary to think we save our feelings of excitement for sporting events and put God only in the category of obligation?

In his lifetime Jesus was hardly a boring person. Thousands followed him. Individuals cried out to him, throngs cheered him, sinners wept over him and many of his first followers died for him. What was the energy that they felt?

Have we who preached him made him boring? Have we, who say we believe in him, really allowed ourselves to feel his presence in our lives? Have we allowed ourselves an intellectual faith that touches our minds, but not an emotional faith that leads us to risk our lives for him as did many of the saints?

Again, I make all of these statements without any intention of hidden criticism of anyone. I make them out of a genuine search for truth. I want a faith built on intellectually defensible doctrines. Emotion without meaning is not attractive to me.

Yet would it not be a sad commentary if we went to our graves having to admit that we were more excited about a Cal Ripken home run than we were about the presence of Christ in the Blessed Sacrament? Will we have to admit at the end of life that we longed for vacations more than we longed to spend time in prayer? Must we admit then that we worked harder for a new car than we ever worked to make God better known to others?

God loves us with an eternal love. He is willing to forgive our worst offenses and to heal our worst hurts. He was willing to die for us to prove his love and even to promise that if we believe in him, we would not stay dead. He promised us not only his own joy but even his own Spirit.

We humans can actually be like God. How could I not be excited about that?

Wouldn't it be wonderful if, right now, I just gave myself the time to realize how wonderful God is and how wonderful he is to me? Wouldn't it be wonderful if the thought of God never bored anyone again?

Every Baby
Deserves a Birthday

■

She's a young mother with four children already, and she just found out that she's pregnant again. In a state of panic she called a girlfriend.

"Get rid of it!" her friend counseled. "You have children already. You and your husband are not getting along that well. There's a little place up the road. I'll go with you."

"But I couldn't live with myself if I did that," the young mother replied.

She called another girlfriend. "Look," her friend said, "why bring another child into the world when it might not really be loved by your husband? Right now, it's only hair and fingernails! Do something right away. I'll go to the hospital with you."

The story I have just told is true. While disguising some details, I have recounted the conversations as the young mother told them to me.

The people she talked to were not bad people. They were friends. They honestly wanted to help her. Sadly, like the counselors of Job in the Bible, they brought more anxiety than help.

The mother in question decided to have the baby. Her reasoning was simple and unpretentious. "It was against my principles," she said. "I always say to my girls not to get pregnant because I'm not going to help them have an abortion. If they get pregnant, they're going to have to have the baby. Now, I have to practice what I preach."

While acknowledging that her marriage had been shaky, she replied to her friends who said that this was not a good situation to bring a new life into, "But would you kill one of your children just because you and your husband were having a hard time?" I was stunned by the power of that sentence.

She continued, "I look around at my kids, and I realize that's exactly what I would be doing. Which one of my children would I want not to be alive just because our marriage isn't perfect?

"I realized that if I had an abortion, every time I saw a baby I would feel guilty. I knew that it would not stop with babies. As the years would pass, I would see 2- and 3- and 5-year-olds and on and on, and I would know that my baby would be that age. I would wonder what the child would have been like."

I tell this woman's story, not to make people who have had abortions feel guilty. God forgives our worst sins, and we need to forgive ourselves our worst choices. As I have said before, the woman is also a victim when an abortion is performed.

I tell this story, however, because it helps to highlight the pressure many women are under to have abortions. Abortions are legal, and it's easy to forget that something legally right may not be morally right.

Abortions are convenient, and so there is great pressure to act quickly without thinking thoroughly. There are many reasons why friends, and even family, will help us justify having an abortion, thus increasing the pressure.

There is the lure of controlling one's own body and making one's own choices, forgetting that now there is another body involved and another life that deserves a choice.

And did you notice in the advice she was given by friends how the new life was referred to as "it?" It's so much easier to kill "fingernails and hair," to kill an "it," than to realize that we are killing a developing human being.

One doctor she went to did advise her strongly against abortion, "I'm sorry," the doctor said, "but I'm Catholic. I could never advise an abortion. My husband is a pathologist, and he sees many of these aborted fetuses. Even at three months they are well-developed. There's a person there."

I like to think of that young mother as one of life's heroes. She is not a religious fanatic. She is not attempting to force her values on anyone else.

But she does have values. And she dares to live them, at no small personal cost to herself. And a new life will be born. And the husband may yet learn to love the new child.

And one day a little child somewhere will be blowing out candles on a cake and others will be singing and presents will be wrapped. And you and I will know the rest of the story, a story about a mother who believed the saying, "Every baby deserves a birthday."

An Accident Can Drive You Crazy

My column about my speeding ticket elicited a number of responses, but unfortunately, no one sent any checks to help pay the fine. Misery may love company but not love it that much, apparently.

My favorite response, however, came in the form of this list of quotes that were actually taken from insurance forms. When people have accidents, they are often asked to summarize in a few words exactly what happened. Here are a few of the summaries:

"Coming home, I drove into the wrong house and collided with a tree I don't have."

"The other car collided with mine without giving warning of its intentions."

"I thought my window was down, but I found out it was up when I put my hand through it."

"I collided with a stationary truck coming the other way."

"A truck backed through my windshield into my wife's face."

"A pedestrian hit me and went under my car."

"The guy was all over the road. I had to swerve a number of times before I hit him."

"I pulled away from the side of the road, glanced at my mother-in-law and headed over the embankment."

"In my attempt to kill a fly, I drove into a telephone pole."

"I had been shopping for plants all day and was on my way home. As I reached an intersection, a hedge sprang up obscuring my vision. I did not see the other car."

"I have been driving my car for forty years when I fell asleep at the wheel and had an accident."

"I was on my way to the doctor's office with rear end trouble when my universal joint gave way causing me to have an accident."

"As I approached the intersection, a stop sign suddenly appeared in a place where no stop sign had ever appeared before. I was unable to stop in time to avoid the accident."

"To avoid hitting the bumper of the car in front, I struck the pedestrian."

"My car was legally parked as it backed into the other vehicle."

"An invisible car came out of nowhere, struck my vehicle and vanished."

"I told the police that I was not injured, but on removing my hat, I found that I had a skull fracture."

"I was sure the old fellow would never make it to the other side of the roadway when I hit him."

"The pedestrian had no idea which direction to go so I ran over him."

"I saw the slow-moving, sad-faced old gentleman as he bounced off the hood of my car."

"I was thrown from my car as it left the road. I was later found in a ditch by some stray cows."

"The telephone pole was approaching fast. I was attempting to swerve out of its path when it struck my front end."

"I was unable to stop in time, and my car crashed into the vehicle. The driver and passenger then left immediately for a vacation with injuries."

The Classic
Works Of God

It's fun to read again some of the classics of literature that I had to read in high school and college. Recently, I reread "The Odyssey," the heroic story of Odysseus, which was written some 3,000 years ago by the blind bard Homer.

Troy lay in ashes, and the victorious Greek warriors had long ago sailed home, all except Odysseus, the hero-king who was condemned to roam the seas, challenged by both gods and men.

This time, however, I read between the lines, looking for quotations indicating how life was viewed and lived 3,000 years ago. Here are a few observations:

The god Zeus is speaking, "What a lamentable thing it is that men should blame the gods and regard us as the source of their troubles, when it is their own wickedness that brings them sufferings worse than any the destiny allots them." Amazing, isn't it? Don't we still blame God when things go wrong?

When the goddess Athena intervenes to help Odysseus, she always comes as a human being. Isn't this what God really did when he took on flesh and blood and was born in Bethlehem?

Men told women what to do. Telemachus, the son of Odysseus, orders his own mother around, "Go to your quarters, and attend to your own work, the loom and the spindle. ... Talking must be men's concern. I am master in this house." It sounded something like St. Paul telling women to be quiet in the assembly. Fortunately, Jesus treated women much better and raised their status to equality.

Zeus says, "However far a man may have strayed, a friendly god could bring him home safely." Doesn't this sound a lot like the story of the Prodigal Son?

"Nausicaa, how did your mother come to have a lazy daughter? Look at the clothing you allow to lie about neglected." This line offers some comfort to parents. Even 3,000 years ago, parents couldn't get their children to clean their rooms or do their chores.

"They lifted the clothes, dropped them into the river and trod them briskly in the troughs." Makes you appreciate the washing machine, doesn't it?

Odysseus meets the souls of the dead and unsuccessfully tries to hug his mother's spirit. She replies, "We no longer have sinews keeping bones and flesh together, but once the life force has departed from our bones, the soul slips away like a dream and flutters on the air."

Odysseus talks to the spirit of Achilles, "For you, Achilles, death should have lost its sting." Remember St. Paul, "Death, where is your victory? Death, where is your sting?"

Obviously, there were many more quotable lines. I was constantly impressed with how this pagan myth so anticipated the Christian religion.

Meditation on
the Lord's Prayer

My most requested sermon is my meditation on the Lord's Prayer. Here is a greatly condensed version of that meditation.

The Lord's Prayer, the Our Father, is a prayer we say so routinely, and often rush through so quickly, that it's easy to miss the meaning of the prayer. Yet, in these troubled times, and in all times, I believe that in the Our Father we have helps for dealing with feelings of inferiority, depression, anxiety, guilt, resentment and fear.

Let's go through the prayer, phrase by phrase, and let the prayer work its miracle for us.

"Our Father, who art in heaven, hallowed be thy name" is the phrase that cures us of any sense of inferiority. To call God Father is to call ourselves his sons and daughters. We are made in God's image – good, wonderful, unique, special people.

As the little boy said, "God made me, and God don't create junk." God could have created a world without you and me, but that wasn't the kind of world God wanted. God wants us here. Never doubt your purpose or your worth! God is our Father, and if God is for us, who can be against us?

"Thy kingdom come, thy will be done on earth as it is in heaven." This is the phrase that can help us with feelings of depression. Once we we are assured of our worth and dignity as sons and daughters of God, then we work to restore someone else's dignity. One of the greatest ways I have found to relieve my own feelings of depression is to get out of myself and go help someone else.

To put it in other words, one of the greatest cures for my depression is to help someone else free him- or herself from oppression. When we dare to care about someone else, when we move from focus on self to focus on others, we find the heaviness in our hearts lifting. We build God's kingdom by building up each other.

"Give us this day our daily bread" is the cure for our anxiety. God will give us whatever it takes to make it through the day. God may not give us things, but God will give us ideas. God will give us energy. God will give us dreams when life seems like a nightmare.

I'll never forget a lady who was divorced, raising three children alone, going to school full time and working full time, saying to me, "Whenever I felt overwhelmed, God put angels on my path. When I didn't know what course to take, someone would advise me. When I couldn't find a baby-sitter, someone would call or offer help. God put angels on my path."

We need not be anxious. God will give us whatever it takes to make it each day. God will put angels on our paths.

"Forgive us our trespasses" frees us from guilt. When we ask forgiveness, God forgives. No sin is unforgivable. No sin is bigger than God. We may need to ask others' forgiveness. We may have to forgive ourselves. But we never have to doubt God's forgiveness. God frees us from sin so that we can get on with the important business of life, loving and caring about each other.

"As we forgive those who trespass against us." This is the phrase that frees us from bitterness and resentment. God's forgiveness frees us from guilt. Our forgiveness of others frees us from resentment and bitterness. If we are holding on to past hurts, holding on to feelings of revenge, the person we are hurting is not the person we are angry at.

The person we are hurting is our self. Forgiving someone does not mean condoning abuse. We have to stand up for our dignity. Forgiving someone else means not punishing ourselves by keeping angry and hurt feelings alive inside us.

"Lead us not into temptation, but deliver us from evil" is our cure for fear. The forces of evil are real and cruel. Life is not always fair, but God always is fair. Sadness and sickness and tragedy and death will not have the last word. Joy and healing and hope and life will have the last word because God writes the last sentence in the Book of Life. God is stronger than all the forces of evil.

God is the Good Shepherd leading us through dark valleys. God is the Prodigal Father, waiting longingly for his child to come home. God is Jesus defending us the way he defended the woman caught in adultery from the stones of others' cruel judgments. God is on our side, and we're going to make it through life.

I hope as you say the Our Father each day, or many times each day, that you will let the meaning and the power of the prayer come alive in your heart.

Ultimately, the Our Father is not just a prayer but an attitude toward life and a way of life. It's a prayer that not only leads us to God but makes us like God. We can let go and let God, "For the kingdom, the power and the glory are yours, now and forever."

AUGUST ■

Vengeance Is Whose?

Do we really think that killing someone "legally" is going to teach others not to kill? It's similar to a parent hitting a child in order to teach the child to stop hitting his little brother.

Curiously, many people use God to justify their own desire for revenge. We often hear them say something like, "The Bible says 'an eye for an eye and a tooth for a tooth.'"

In other passages of the Bible, the Psalms in particular, we read, "He [God] smashes the children's heads against the rocks." Fortunately, we don't go out smashing children's heads against the rocks just because the Bible says so.

The irony remains that the eye for an eye and tooth for a tooth was originally incorporated as an act of mercy.

God was teaching us that if someone stole a sheep, you could not kill him. You could take his sheep but not his life. If a man killed someone, you could not kill his whole family. Only he could die.

How ironic. A refinement of mercy has become a justification for revenge. Unfortunately, when the state participates in justifying taking a life, we all reduce ourselves to the level of street gangs, of terrorists, of feuding groups around the world. They all justify their actions similarly.

A further irony, especially for Christians, is that Jesus went beyond the old law. He said to forgive your enemies, to love your persecutors, to show mercy as our Father has shown mercy to us – the same Father who lets "the rain fall upon the good and the bad alike." If we want to justify taking someone else's life in the name of God, surely that cannot be the Christian God.

I'm not trying to be holier than thou on this issue. I get just as angry, just as incensed at the atrocities that some people perpetrate on others as anyone else does. I know the feeling of "wanting to fry that guy."

But that's just the point. Our anger and passion make us the equal of the murderer, not better! No one has said it better than Martin Luther King, "The thing wrong with an eye for an eye is that everyone ends up blind."

Catching Teens
in the Act

■

Teenagers don't get told enough how good they are. Allow me to share a few stories.

I was standing in line at a McDonald's one day behind three teenagers. (Notice that I dine at only the finest restaurants.) They were being pretty typical teenage boys, joking around, loud and friendly.

When they received their order and paid for it, I noticed one of the teenagers, instead a putting the change in his pocket, deposited it in a little container on the counter for the Ronald McDonald House. He didn't call any attention to what he had done, and the three of them just walked away.

As I watched that scene, I began thinking that if that teenager had pulled a gun and held up the McDonald's, the story would have been on every newscast in the city. A teenager giving some money to help someone else rarely gets noticed. I just wanted teenagers to know that people do notice the good they do.

My second story comes from Mount St. Joe's High School where I had the privilege of celebrating one of the Ash Wednesday services. When I had finished preaching, two students came to the podium.

The first told the assembled student body about the time he had spent in Bolivia at a Xaverian Mission. He spoke of the poverty of the people, about their lives with no television, no radio, no stereos, none of the luxuries we consider necessities. He noted the simplicity and joy of those poor people and invited his fellow students to help in any way possible.

The next student thanked the rest of the student body for the many bags of clothes they had donated, which he and some other students had delivered to Bea Gaddy to be given to the poor. He spoke of the people who had lined up early in the day to get food and clothing.

That scene of social concern and involvement is repeated in so many Catholic high schools and grade schools and confirmation classes and religious education programs. But how rarely we hear the story. A teenager buying or selling drugs is news. Teenagers feeding the hungry or clothing the naked seem to go unnoticed.

The final scene I want to share occurred at the Journalism Workshop and Awards ceremony sponsored by *The Catholic Review*. Here were many students from our area high schools going to workshops on writing and photography and layout. Here were many teenagers involved in editing and designing school newspapers and providing pictures and features and editorials for those papers.

Since I had the honor of handing out the awards, I took the time to read the entries. The articles were well-written, articulate, challenging, insightful and humorous. We hear so often of teenagers being the victims of peer pressure, but here were teens who were exerting peer pressure for the good.

While not everyone received an award, I believe each of those teens was a winner. Each was a winner over laziness ("It's too much trouble"), a winner over peer pressure ("What will others think?"), a winner over apathy ("I'll let someone else worry about it").

In reality teens are just like us, developing human beings, seeking to make the world better and seeking to make their lives make a difference. Like us, teens need the Gospel and the church to inspire and guide them. Teens also need to be "caught" doing good.

The Friends We Haven't Met

Too little attention, I believe, has been paid to the love between brothers and sisters. In the recent hostage release I was constantly impressed by the role that sisters of the hostages played.

It was Terry Anderson's sister who almost single-handedly kept his name before the American public, kept his plight before the government, kept the issue alive when it was so easy to forget.

Parents are amazed to watch their children fight and "kill" each other at home and then become very protective of each other outside the home. At Christmas time, a little boy was sitting on Santa Claus' lap, and Santa asked him if he had been naughty.

The little boy said no but then looked at his mother and looked back at Santa and said, "Well, I did sit on my sister's head and twist her arm." I think of that book of letters that children wrote to God. One of my favorites has always been, "Dear God: Maybe Cain and Abel wouldn't kill each other so much if they had their own rooms. It works for me and my brother."

One of the blessings that I have always cherished in my life is my relationship with my sister Helen. Helen started out as my "big" sister, but my hair started graying and hers kept staying the same so I became the "older" brother.

Other things changed too. When I was first ordained, people would meet her and say, "Oh, you're Father Joe's sister." Now whenever I meet any educators, especially in Baltimore County, someone says, "Oh, you're Helen Eder's brother."

Over the years, though, we have always been there for each other. Through growing up and growing older, through family crises and burying parents, through doubts and certainties, when all was well and all was not so well, there was always the certainty that someone knew, someone understood, someone cared.

In our society we need more brothers and sisters. For many reasons, we are not always close to our siblings, emotionally or geographically. We need to learn the art of creating new "families" wherever we are. We need another model for men and women to interact with each other, other than the sexual model. It is not by accident that the United States is the loneliest nation on earth. We often isolate ourselves from others and then expect our spouse to meet all of our needs. When he or she is not able to be all things to us, we often become frustrated.

What we need to do is to rediscover friendship. We need to realize that while we can be sexually committed to one person for life, we obviously need a wider circle of friends. Father Andrew Greeley discovered years ago in his research that women who had close friendships with priests also had better relationships with their husbands.

As a society, we need to grow more secure within ourselves so that we do not interpret a spouse's need for friendship with members of the opposite sex as an indication that we have somehow failed. We also do not need to interpret someone spending time with a member of the opposite sex as an affair.

Let's face it. Many of our relationships with co-workers are superficial. Many of our family members, if we have family members, are scattered over various distances. Many of the people with whom we interact on a daily basis are merely acquaintances.

If we can find a "soul mate," someone that we can share our thoughts and feelings and joys and sorrows with, then we have found the "pearl of great price."

When the apostles asked Jesus what they would get if they left all to follow him, Jesus promised a hundredfold of "mothers, brothers, sisters

– family." Once we leave behind our possessive relationships, leave behind our need to control someone else, we then open ourselves to the capacity of establishing relationships with many people. Christian relationships, based not on lust, power or the need to control but on respect, understanding, appreciation and care, can radically change us and change our world.

The problem is not that we are lonely. The problem is that we are surrounded by brothers and sisters whom we have yet to meet.

Life & Death
& ECMs

It was the most terrifying moment of my driving experience. As I drove down Merritt Boulevard in Dundalk, in traffic, at approximately 35 mph, suddenly my steering column locked and my brakes failed! Being on the inside lane next to a grass median strip, my car miraculously drifted out of traffic and came to a halt.

Trembling, I restarted my car, and the steering was fine and the brakes worked. I gingerly drove my car to a nearby garage and after a computer analysis, was told that my ECM (Electronic Control Module) was not working properly. Put simply, when part of the car's computer – the ECM – fails, the car loses all power immediately and without warning.

In addition to my personal fright, I immediately became incensed at the thought of how many accidents have gone undetected as a result of failing Electronic Control Modules.

I had only to think back to two weeks prior when I had driven with my sister from Baltimore to Kentucky to visit our three aunts who are Ursuline nuns. Had my car gone off the road while driving 65 mph through the mountains of West Virginia, no doubt the cause of my death and my sister's death would have been reported something like, "The driver lost control of his car while negotiating a turn at high speeds."

No one would have even heard of, much less investigated, an Electronic Control Module failure. During the last 70 miles of that trip, from Lexington to Louisville, we were caught in torrential rains that made driving treacherous. Had my Electronic Control Module failed at that point and had I plowed into the car in front of me, no doubt the accident would have been written off as "slick pavement" or "poor visibility due to rain." But my sister and I, and possibly a lot of other folks, might have been killed or injured in a chain-reaction collision.

While I can't pretend to understand all the high technology that goes into modern cars, one thing is patently clear. To build an automobile that can lose all power, including steering and brakes, without warning, is obscene!

Think for a minute. How many stories have we heard of cars crossing median strips and crashing into oncoming traffic? If I had been driving at 60 mph on I-95 and my ECM had failed, I would have had no choice. Remember, with no power, which includes no steering and no brakes, the car controls you. Any lawyer currently defending a client involved in an automobile accident would be a fool not to consider computer error.

To add insult to injury, when my problem was diagnosed, a mechanic commented, "They've been having a lot of trouble with that." "That" was not exactly a sticking window or a squeak in the brakes. "That" was a life-threatening defect with no recall notices, no manufacturer warnings, no announcements as to the potential hazards.

No doubt, though, the auto manufacturers will hasten to assure you it is "no big deal." Their public relations divisions will comfort you, "Sorry to hear about the death or injury of your loved one or friend, but, well, driving is dangerous. We do make better commercials even if we don't make better cars. Maybe we'll even find a clergyman to tell you that the death or injury was "God's will."

It's always easier to blame God for our selfish decisions. And a lot cheaper too.

Encountering God
Can Be the Simplest
Thing in the World

I saw her standing there in church. Her left arm was outstretched, as her left hand held the hand of a statue of Jesus. Her lips moved quietly as she stared intently at the face of Jesus. Then she walked away.

Treatises have been written on prayer. I doubt if that woman has read any of them. All she did was hold the hand of Jesus as she spoke to him. It didn't seem very complicated. It just seemed a very natural thing to do.

Was she worshiping a statue, as some people charge? No. She was worshiping the God beyond the image. The image drew her to God. The cold stone helped bring her into the heart of the living God.

Perhaps we who deal with the complexities of life and of religion sometimes miss the fact that life is pretty simple for many people. To the question of the meaning of life, they have not found a better answer than the old catechism answer that "God made me to know, love and serve him in this life and to be happy with him forever in the next."

Life is a journey. The commandments of God and of the church guide our way. The Eucharist provides nourishment for the journey. The sacraments are signs of God's presence, blessing, forgiving and healing us on our way to the kingdom.

The sacramentals are important to such people. The sacramentals are signs of the divine in tangible and touchable form.

Dipping our hands into holy water and signing ourselves with the sign of the Cross reminds us that we have been reborn through the waters of baptism and saved by the cross of Christ. Lighting candles reminds us of our faith in Christ, the Light of the world.

The rosary becomes a form of meditation and prayer that links us with the mysteries of Christ's life and helps to make sense out of our own lives. Medals and the like become symbols of Christ and his Mother and the saints that we wear around our necks or attached to clothing to symbolize that we "have put on Christ," whose "yoke is sweet and burden light."

Statues of Christ and Mary and the saints are like family pictures that we keep around our church home to remind us of other members of the family who have lived well before us.

Life is getting more complex day by day. Yet in the midst of complexity, maybe we need to return to simplicity. We need to remind ourselves that God will reveal himself to his people in many ways. If we make religion too complicated for people, we risk making it seem that God is too mysterious for people.

Some of the greatest saints have discovered that it is not what we say about God but what we feel about God that matters. I believe it was Thomas a Kempis who wrote, "I would rather feel compunction than know how to spell it."

Again, St. Thomas Aquinas, a saint and doctor of the church who devoted his life to writing about God and belief in God, at the end of his life supposedly said, "All of my writings are as so much straw."

No one can exhaust the mystery of God. That's why the answer to questions about God often comes from those of simple faith rather than those of complicated faith. As St. John Chrysostom once said, "The more insignificant your brother is the more Christ comes to you in him."

Yes, I will write and talk again about prayer. But I'm not sure I will say anything better than the little lady who held the hand of Christ, stared at his face and just spoke to him in her own words. Maybe there is nothing more to say.

What Does the Religious Life Really Mean?

■

The past few months have been part of the "season of anniver-saries." How casually many of us have noted the 25th or 50th anniversary of service of some priest or religious. Yet have we ever wondered what it means to "give our lives to God?"

I thought of that as I watched the priests celebrating anniversaries process in for their Jubilee Mass. Here were the men of pre-Vatican II and post-Vatican II. Here were the men who weathered Humanae Vitae (the birth control encyclical) and liturgical changes and identity crises and increased work and worries.

Here were the men who were still here, still faithful, still dedicated. Here were the men of whom no book will likely be written but men whose very lives compose a volume of praise and fidelity to God.

What does it mean to give your life to God? I thought of that last month as I shared in the celebration with Sister Edward Thomas at St. Joseph's Hospital. [Sister Edward Thomas is just one of thousands of priests and religious who came to these shores from the distant shores of Ireland.] Sister Edward celebrated 50 years of service to the sick and pained and desperate.

I think those who work in the medical field often labor in an obscurity that others do not share.

After all who does not remember their parish priest as they were growing up? Who cannot recount stories of their favorite nun from grade school?

Yet who remembers the Sister in the emergency room or on the hospital ward?

I tried to imagine just how many people Sister Edward Thomas might have touched in her lifetime. If she ministered to just 50 patients a day, a conservative estimate given her standards, she would personally have touched over a million people in her life.

Yet even that is not a fair measurement. Who can count the people she touched who touched others? What about the discouraged priest she may have encouraged to remain a priest? What of the other professionals who were better professionals because of her supervision? What of the other religious who were supported in their ministries by her?

In trying to envision all the lives touched by all of the people celebrating anniversaries this year, an interesting scene came to mind. I recalled the immense throngs who flocked to see the pope at his every stop in the United States.

Suddenly, it became clear to me that, while the pope received the cheers, he was a symbol of all of these anonymous good people who touched all of those people cheering. He was a symbol of the priest who heard the confession that reconciled someone to the church. He was a symbol of the religious who taught children respect for the pope as a successor of Peter. He was a symbol of all who ministered to the sick in the name of the church.

In my fantasies, I would like for just a moment to assemble such a crowd on the Mall in Washington or in Chicago or in Memorial Stadium here. Then I would want to put Sister Edward Thomas in the middle and let her receive the cheers for just a few moments. It would be a token symbol of all the people she touched. Still it would be a moment.

Yet she, and so many like her, would refuse such an idea. They are more accustomed to serving than being applauded. In their lives that work has been long and the cheers few.

All who minister in Christ's name know the same was true of Christ. When he was providing food and miracles, the crowds were large. When he spoke of the need to change lives, the crowds dwindled. Only one leper came back to say thanks because all wanted to be cured but only one wanted to be changed.

Ultimately, the world did not really know what Jesus was all about. Our world does not really know what these people who "gave their lives for God" are all about either. As Mother Theresa said so well, "We are not called to be successful. We are called to be faithful."

I am reminded of the parable about the man going through Sodom and Gomorrah shouting for repentance. Someone stopped him and said, "Why are you shouting so loud? These people don't want to change." The prophet replied, "I'm shouting so loud hoping to keep these people from changing me."

To all those who have shouted God with their lives, we say thanks. Thanks for giving your lives to God, and in the process, bringing God into our lives. To Sister Edward Thomas our thanks extends all the way from here to the shores of Ireland. We say thanks to that Emerald Isle that dared to conquer the world for Christ.

SEPTEMBER ▪

Why Not Do
Something About It?

One of the greatest tributes to American ingenuity is how we celebrate work by taking a day off.

Labor Day, which is really summer's swan song, is an opportune moment to ask, "What efforts really make a difference in life?" Most of us are stuck with the reality of working for a living, but how many of us ever ask what makes the world a better place to live in?

Many people experience a powerlessness about making a real difference in life. The standard complaint is "somebody should do something about that," but we presume the "somebody" is someone else. What would happen if you and I decided to dare to do something that made a difference?

One idea was suggested by a public service commercial I heard recently. The commercial said something like, "Alone, there's not much any one of us can do. But what would happen if 230 million of us did something? Suppose every person in the United States pledged five percent of their income and five hours of their time each week to some cause they believed in?"

What an enormous army of energy and resources such an idea could produce!

Think of the students tutored, drug addicts aided, handicapped helped, nursing homes visited, religion classes taught and dying people comforted.

Think of the volunteers for hospice and hospitals, for parishes and prisons, for eucharistic ministers and home visitors.

Think what it would mean to our parish churches if parishioners went from their current average contribution of 1.1 percent to 2.2 percent (the average Protestant contribution). Individuals could donate the remaining 2.8 percent of their contribution to the Propagation of the Faith, to health organizations, to UNICEF or to a host of other worthwhile charities.

Do we have the will to make such a commitment? Obviously, there are people who cannot afford such a commitment. Yet, I'm inclined to think that their number is limited. If we look at the staggering amounts of money spent on cigarettes, on alcohol, on pornography, on conveniences, on luxuries, it's hard to imagine that the money is not there to give.

As one of my grade school teachers always said, "Where there's a will, there's a way."

In life it is always easier to complain about what is not being done than it is to offer to do what I can do. It is always easier to make excuses than it is to make time.

It is always easier to confuse what I want with what I need. It is always easier to look out for myself than to care about others.

Yet, the easy way is seldom the Christ way. Christ modeled giving all of himself to others in hopes that we would give some of ourselves to others.

Labor Day is the beginning of the real new year. The calendar changes in January, but life changes in September. Schools open again. Meetings start again. Parish activities pick up again.

Is now not a good time to make a resolution for the new year? Is now not a good time to begin a labor of love, of committing five percent of our income and five hours of our time weekly to something we believe in?

We all know the reasons why we can't. Will we dare to find reasons why we can?

The Crow of an Angel

When was the last time you heard a rooster crow in a funeral home? Let me tell you a story.

Recently I received a phone call from a young lady whose grandmother had just died. The granddaughter explained that her grandmother was a devoted listener to my weekly radio show on WPOC. She told me how she had put earphones on her grandmother in the hospital so she could listen to my show for the last time on the Sunday before she died.

One of her grandmother's requests was that I be invited to participate in her funeral. Fortunately, the morning requested was available. Father Daniel Free, the Passionist priest who is the chaplain at St. Agnes Hospital, had heard the lady's confession and reconciled her to the church before she died. He was also requested to share the service.

Father Free and I divided the service between us. The family had only requested prayers at the funeral home. As Father Free finished the first reading and was just beginning the Responsorial Psalm, it happened. "Cock-a-doodle-doo" sounded in the funeral home.

A rooster was crowing. It crowed again. The whole congregation burst into laughter. All eyes were fixed on the coffin. The reading abruptly stopped. Then, between the crows, I heard a voice, "It is 9:30," and the crowing continued.

Then I realized that grandmom was wearing a talking and crowing wrist watch! The crowing continued for a full minute with no way to stop it. By the time it had finished, everyone was sufficiently amused and relaxed so that it was possible for many family members and friends to share some very tender thoughts about Margaret.

I tell this story for several reasons. First, because it was, without a doubt, the strangest thing that ever happened to me in a funeral home. Second, I tell it because the incident highlighted the kind of warm and caring relationship that existed between this woman, her six children, her 12 grandchildren and, I think, one great-grandchild.

This particular woman would probably have been classified by church sociologists as one of the 80 million unchurched people living in our country. In her defense, I want to emphasize that "unchurched" does not necessarily mean "un-faith-filled."

Misunderstandings run long and deep. Yet, while we continue to make our churches more welcoming and hospitable for all, it is also beautiful to recognize that God never forgets his people. When I saw the kind of love in that family, it was obvious to me that God was with this woman and in this woman.

Just as Domino's can deliver pizza wherever we are, God also delivers love wherever we are. I believe we are called not just to bring God to people but to bring God out in people. We are called to recognize divinity.

One final thought. I have a fantasy that someone may be walking by or through Louden Park Cemetery late at night. Perhaps they may have had too much to drink or may be on some drug. As they walk through the quietness, suddenly they hear a voice coming from one of the graves saying, "It's midnight."

And then a rooster starts crowing. I have a hunch that person will never take another drink or another drug again. Life does not end with the grave. Neither does love. From her place in heaven, a lady who never spent much time in church will spend eternity with God.

She will be a special guardian angel for all who knew and loved her in life. Here on earth, a voice from the coffin will have the last laugh on all of us. And, I think, God laughs too.

The Superstars
of Life

■

With all due respect to Arnold Schwarzenegger and other body builders, I do not think they are the strongest people in the world. My vote for the world's strongest people goes to parents of young children.

Allow me to explain how I arrived at this conclusion. First, after baptisms, I am often asked by the mother of the baby, "Oh, Father Joe, do you want to hold the baby?" Usually the baby responds, "No, I don't want him to hold me," and immediately bursts into tears.

After about a minute of holding the crying infant, I'm thinking to myself, "Hey, this kid weighs a ton." I'm too embarrassed to say anything because the parents have been holding the baby for hours.

My second piece of research comes from watching parents with children in malls. I can't tell you the number of times I've watched a petite woman push a stroller with one hand, hold another child in her arms, have a third trailing behind her holding onto her coat – and make it through a set of double doors entering a store. Often, I chivalrously hurry to help, but they are usually through by the time I get there.

"How do they do that?" I often wonder to myself.

This research leads me to the conclusion that the Olympics need to get some new contests that measure strength in the real world. After all, how many times in your life have you really needed to run 26 miles? How many times have you really needed to lift 500 or 600 pounds over your head?

So why not measure something that matters? Why not have the musclemen of the world see how many children they can carry at once? Why not measure how long it takes to find children lost in a store? Why not have a contest timing how long it takes to fold a stroller, put it in the trunk and buckle the kids in their car seats?

I would ignore the professional athletes each time. I'd bet every time on parents of young children.

Beyond the physical strength of parents, I also want to salute their emotional and spiritual strength. I don't think there's any job on earth more difficult than raising children. I also think no job on earth is more noble.

No, I'm certainly not trying to devalue virginity or celibacy for the sake of the kingdom. I'm not trying to make single people or childless couples feel worse than they often do. I think we childless people need to realize we give life any time we care about someone else.

A final thought about single parents. Some of the greatest heroism currently going on in our society today is the heroism required to raise children without a spouse at home. Every day I see single parents working extra hours, going to school to improve skills, finding babysitters, struggling to find day care – in short, killing themselves to give their children the best they can give them. Don't tell me about the "super-stars" who drive in a run in the ninth inning or kick a winning field goal with three seconds left.

The real superstars of life are those parents working to beat the odds, working to make ends meet. One important thought for these parents. In the Scriptures, Joseph, the foster father of Jesus, is not present in Jesus' adult life. Apparently he died some time earlier. This leads me to conclude that Jesus, Son of God and Savior of the world, spent some period of his life in a single-parent family.

If a single-parent family was good enough for God, it will be good enough for your children. In our darkest hours, don't forget to turn to Mary, the Mother of God, in prayer. She knows what it's like to be a single parent too.

Theology of
The Big Toe

◾

In 12 years of seminary training, I never took a course entitled "The Theology of the Big Toe." Maybe such a course should be mandatory.

Recently I had the misfortune of tripping while I was out walking, resulting in a "jammed" or "sprained" toe. It was painful to put on a sock or shoe, much less walk. I learned a lot from that experience.

First, I learned that a toe injury is an injury that elicits little compassion. "So your toe hurts, huh? That's too bad. People are starving, and you're worried about your toe." My only response was to paraphrase that commercial for Travelers Checks – "Your toe! Try to leave home without it!"

Second, I realized how easy it is to take for granted all the things that go right in life. I can honestly say that I don't ever remember kneeling down at night and saying, "Thank you, God, that my toe felt good today." When something is going right, we never think about it. When a toe is doing fine, we never think about it. When a toe is excruciatingly painful, it's difficult to concentrate on anything else.

A wise spiritual writer once said, if the only prayer we ever said was "Thank you, Lord," we would be holy people. On any given day there is so much more to be thankful for than to be sad about. The fact that we are alive is a good place to start.

If a body part is hurting, we can be grateful that most parts are working fine. If we have lost a loved one, we can be grateful that not all of our loved ones have died, that not all the people who care about us are gone. If we have failed in some area, it does not make us failures in life. Beginning and ending the day in prayerful gratitude for what we have puts every pain and loss in perspective.

A third thing I learned from my spirituality of the toe is a reaffirmation of the idea of the Mystical Body of Christ. As St. Paul said, we are all members of the Body of Christ. Yet it's easy to forget who's important, isn't it? Jesus said the one who serves is most important. When we see beautiful church services of pageantry and pomp, it's easy to forget who cleaned the church, who put the lights in the sockets, who fixed the door knobs and door handles.

When we see a presidential motorcade, do we wonder who changed the oil in the president's car? who vacuumed it? who changed the tires? When we see the important people of life dining at restaurants, do we ever wonder who fixed the salad? who washed the dishes? who will empty the trash?

A big toe is a seemingly unimportant part of the body. But try to walk without it. Try to have a church service without lights or drive a car without oil or eat on dirty dishes. It doesn't take long to realize that "important" is a relative term.

One final thought: any kind of minor injury slows us down. I like to walk fast, to move quickly, to get where I need to go. It's difficult, slowing down. But life has a way of slowing all of us down. There comes a time when age or illness or injury will limit our mobility.

The minor interruptions to our pace of life prepare us for the final interruption: "Be still and know I am God." If we can be still and just be with God now, it's not a bad preparation for being with God forever.

When our compulsive drive to be busy is stilled, we realize that God loves us for who we are, not for what we do.

The Fruits of Ministry Ripen at a Block Party

They say you can't go back again, but I tried anyway. I went back to Parklawn Avenue, a street just two blocks below the Shrine of the Little Flower parish in East Baltimore. The neighbors were having a block party, and a couple of people had invited me to come by.

I, of course, had been by this area on various occasions since I had left the parish as an associate pastor nearly 15 years before. Yet this seemed like an official visit. This was a chance to see everybody again if just for an evening.

As I turned down the block, everybody seemed to be there. Adults stood on the sidewalks or sat on porches. Teenagers danced in the street. Children played everywhere. Music blared as a disc jockey spun records. Food seemed to multiply the way the loaves multiplied for another crowd so many years ago.

There were familiar faces among the crowd. Here were the people I had preached to and ministered to. Jane and Joe were there along with Joan. Jane and Charlie were also there.

There was the man whose wife had died too early. Here was the wonderful lady whose son I had buried. There was that cute little red-haired girl who was now a cute red-haired adult.

There was Frank, who remembered my visit in the hospital. "It was snowing like crazy that day and I asked you what you were doing on a day like that and you said it was easier to drive when no one else was on the road."

Priestly ministry is sometimes like walking through water. You do what you do and wonder if it made any difference. It was nice to know that someone remembered. Peggy came over for a hug and told me some things she remembered too.

Slowly, like uninvited guests, dark clouds began to move in, and then suddenly they dumped their contents on the party-goers below. Desserts were covered, and salads were rushed to safety. Frank gave me an umbrella to allow me to continue my visiting, and Andy and his wife and the good sisters invited me to wait out the storm on their porch – along with a beer and some food. Hospitality has always been a trademark of the neighborhood.

There were some poignant conversations as well. One man said to his neighbor, "I had a lump in my throat tonight as I watched you give out communion."

Another man explained, "I'm not supposed to be here. I have cancer." Yet he was here, and the world seemed better for it.

"We have such wonderful young people moving into the neighborhood," said a wonderful older person. Instead of resentment of the young, here was a neighborhood that welcomed a new generation.

I felt many emotions tugging at me as I experienced that evening. I was delighted to be with so many genuine, caring people.

I was also humbled by the aging process. Here were many children who did not even exist when I last walked that neighborhood as a parish priest. Here were the young people who had existed then, now with children of their own. Life goes on. Neighborhoods get recycled, and so does the world. We are all on this stage of life but a brief moment.

As the evening wore on and the rain continued, I realized it was time to go. Despite the steady downpour on that warm September evening, the young people continued to dance in the streets. The nice thing about being drenched is that you can't get any more drenched. Saturation does have its advantages.

A few more waves to people on porches and a few smiles at the dancers and suddenly I was around the corner and headed toward my car.

It was just a block on Parklawn Avenue, but it could have been any number of blocks in any number of places in East Baltimore.

It was a place where good, unpretentious people lived. It was a place where people still went to church on Sunday and lived their faith the rest of the week. It was a place where the parish priests and sisters were spoken of affectionately.

It was the kind of neighborhood I could imagine that Jesus grew up in. It's the kind of neighborhood he still lives in today.

The Sum of
the Parts

![marker]

Since I wrote "The Theology of The Big Toe," kind people ask me how my toe is. My toe is fine, but my knee is killing me. Remember that old commercial about "trading a headache for an upset stomach?" That's apparently what I have done.

As anyone who has experienced injury understands, when you injure one part of the body, frequently there is other damage, not immediately recognized. X-rays indicated that when I tripped, I not only hurt my toe but traumatized my knee as well. Apparently ligaments have been stretched or otherwise damaged.

Six weeks of limping, rest and anti-inflammatory drugs, and nothing seems to be improving. What a revolting development!

What lessons might we learn from this injury?

The *first*, obviously, is a reaffirmation of the whole concept of the Mystical Body, of the church as the Body of Christ. When one part suffers, all parts suffer.

Part of why the church makes a "preferential option for the poor," why the church runs soup kitchens here and ministers through Catholic Relief Services around the world, is that when anyone hurts, the whole church hurts.

Second, pain can bring out our worst side. I'm aware of my own depression from pain and inactivity. I don't feel like writing or counseling. I don't make my best decisions when I'm hurting.

This aspect is important to remember today when there is so much in the news about "suicide machines" and best-selling books on ending our lives and even legislation moving toward euthanasia. People in pain may choose the ultimate solution when better solutions are available. The world does not need better means to suicide.

Third, being rendered partially helpless helps us to experience how much of our feelings of self-worth come from "doing." I get angry when my body doesn't respond because I have places to go and things to do and people to see.

I don't rest easily. Yet are we most like Christ in our doing or in our helplessness? We know from reading the Scriptures that Jesus visited villages, healed the sick, preached good news and even raised the dead. Yet in his moments of helplessness, when he was hanging on the cross, he redeemed the world. It's hard to believe that our worth comes from what we are, not from what we do. Nothing in society affirms that. But God affirms that.

Fourth, pain sensitizes us to the pain of others. It's extremely humbling not to walk as briskly as I would want to, to take extra precautions crossing the street because I can't move quickly. Suddenly it sensitizes us to the world of people with physical disabilities because of age or illness or accidents. All of us are only "temporarily able-bodied."

A final thought about our being connected as parts of the same body. A toe doesn't seem very important. A knee doesn't get much attention. But when they hurt, they disable the rest of the body.

A lot of times individuals say things like "Hey, if I want to drink, I'm only hurting myself" or "If I want to smoke, I'm only hurting me" or "If I do drugs, that's my decision, not yours." But suddenly we realize that there are no "private" sins. We do influence one another. We can drag each other down. We can inspire each other.

Developing my abilities, being all I can be, is my gift to you. The body and the world work best when each of us is healthy and all of us work together.

Little Pencils of God

"It's easy to find the church," she said. "It's right across from Monahan's bar." I love when people give directions that way.

The presumption is that the bar is likely to be more popular than the church. It reminded me of a time years ago when I asked my physician whether alcohol was good or bad for your health. The good doctor replied, "Well Father, it took us awhile, but eventually we realized that there were more old drunks than old doctors."

The particular church I refer to is St. Luke's United Methodist Church. It's a wonderful church with an able pastor the Rev. David Jones and kind members who host senior citizen meals and socials several times a week. I had been invited to speak to the senior citizens' group, and the young man who introduced me said that he "remembered a day when a Catholic priest wouldn't even set foot in a Methodist church." God's grace works slowly sometimes, but it does work.

It reminded me of another occasion, in another Methodist church. I was assisting the minister in blessing a couple's wedding. In my remarks I happened to mention that a couple of generations back on my mother's side, my family had been Methodist. I commented that I was sure that part of the family was looking down from heaven, pleased that I had finally made it to the right church.

The minister then told an astounding story. He said that in the 18th century a Catholic priest was sailing to America and apparently on the trip from Europe, he fell in love. He married the woman and left the priesthood. The Methodist minister then added that his family research indicated that he was a direct descendent of that man.

From a bar, we find a church. From a Methodist background comes a Catholic priest. From a Catholic background comes a Methodist minister. Do you remember that old saying that "God writes straight with crooked lines?"

In theological terms, we call it Divine Providence. In practical terms, we just say that God will find a way when there seems to be no way.

The scriptural image I keep in mind is that of Jesus standing at the door knocking. On a given day I might not answer the door. On a given day I may be a pretty poor instrument for God to work with. But grace is insistent and relentless. Like the hound of heaven, God really does pursue us "down the labyrinthine ways." God will keep breaking into history, if not through one person, through another; if not one way, then through another; if not in one time, then in another.

We humans upset ourselves so and worry and fret about the darndest things. In the sweep of history many of our worries have a way of working out. Mother Teresa once referred to herself as "a little pencil in the hands of God." In my own life, I fear that God has had to use the eraser more than the lead.

But that's the beauty of faith. God will have his way even if we get in the way. "Be still, and know that I am God." In our quiet, reflective times we know that we write a few sentences, but God always has the last word.

A Modern St. Paul

East Baltimore has a guardian angel. He wanders the streets and back alleys, armed not with the flaming sword of the angel posted outside the Garden of Eden but instead with leaflets of Catholic prayers and medals of the Blessed Mother. He visits the homes of shut-ins, of poor families, of broken individuals and of healthy individuals. Joe Thomas is God's messenger, trying to bring people back to church.

I had the privilege of accompanying Joe on his rounds while I was doing a mini-mission at St. Michael's parish on Wolfe Street. On every corner, in many stores, down back alleys and up main streets, there was the constant greeting of others: "Hi, Mr. Joe." "Thanks for coming by, Mr. Thomas."

I talked to one woman in a store who had not been near a church in years, but she knew Mr. Joe. In one day we visited 22 homes.

Joe Thomas is a member and leader in the Legion of Mary. Their purpose is not only to honor Mary through devotions but to honor Mary through devotion to bringing others back to church.

"I've visited some of these same homes for 15 years," Joe said. "They still haven't returned to church, but I keep visiting." Fifteen years.

Evangelization is a word that few people can pronounce and even fewer can spell. It means bringing God's good news of salvation to others in season and out of season.

In the course of our visits that day, one particular incident stands out. We stopped by to see an old man who lived alone in a dirty, unkempt house. His only companion was his dog. He was a big man. His arms bore tattoos, and his manner was gruff and coarse. He had been away from the church for 50 years.

"In 1983 I was told I was dying, and they asked me if I wanted to see a priest," he said. "'Hell no,' I replied, 'give me a blonde and a bottle of booze.'"

I laughed with him. "I don't blame you," I said. "I'd take a blonde and a bottle of booze over a priest any day."

He seemed comforted that I could identify with him and that I had not come to preach at him. "What kept you away from church all those years?" I asked.

"In 1942," he answered, "my mother died. She died an awful death of cancer. She had been a God-fearing woman all her life, always in church, always saying her prayers. When I saw what happened to her, I said if that's what happens to good people, then I may as well have fun in life."

He paused and then continued thoughtfully, "I guess I was just angry and didn't know what to do with my anger. I guess I got angry at God."

Joe asked him if he wanted to go to confession, and then Joe quietly slipped out of the house. This tough old man then poured out his heart to me.

At the end I'll never forget the tears streaming down his face as his trembling hands held the booklet of Catholic prayers while he prayed the Our Father and made an Act of Contrition. Father Al Illig, the executive director of the Paulist National Catholic Evangelization Association, would have been touched to see one of his publications being put to such good use.

I left the house and went with Joe to visit the lady across the alley. When we emerged from the house, the old man was sitting outside on his steps with his mangy dog. He had come out of the darkness into the light. Joe promised to bring him Holy Communion the next week.

Joe would be back. He always comes back. After having spent 42 years of hard work at Sparrows Point, this "retired" worker for the Lord still has miles to go before he sleeps. With Mary as the love of his life and with Jesus at the heart of his life, Mr. Joe Thomas has found the secret of energy, joy and eternal youth.

Issuing the
"Church Challenge"

Profound thoughts often come in simple sentences.

"I can't imagine anyone going to church every week and not being a better person for it," she said. She is not a theologian or philosopher. She is a very successful business woman who relocated here in Baltimore and immediately began her search for a new church.

"It may be a verse from a hymn or a line in the readings or a sentence from the sermon, but there is always something that you can get out of going to church."

You would not exactly describe this lady as a religious fanatic. "My father died when I was a young adult, and I got so angry at God that I stayed away from church for 10 years," she said. She knows what it's like not to go to church and what it's like going to church, and she concluded that going is better.

Her thoughts inspired in me what I am tempted to call a "Church Challenge." Challenge someone to go to church for four straight weeks and see if it makes a difference. Even better, turn the challenge into an invitation. Invite someone who does not go to church – a family member, a friend, a neighbor – to go to church with you for four straight weeks. All you ask of them is to come with an open mind.

If they're determined not to get anything out of going to church, obviously they won't get anything out of it. An open mind, however, just invites them to be present without prior judgment.

The old prospector used to say, "Gold is where you find it." The same could be said about going to church. There is gold to be mined with pretty minimal effort. We might paraphrase that by saying, "God is where you find him."

So I encourage you to try the "Church Challenge." Parishes might pick a month to invite parishioners to bring someone along. "Try God this month" has worked in various places. Maybe in the fall there could be a campaign entitled "Back to School. Back to Church."

The four weeks of Advent would be a natural time. So would Lent. So would the time after Easter. Any time is a good time.

Let's be honest. We spend a lot more energy on lesser things. We fight the traffic to get to a ball game. When we get to the stadium, we pay top dollar for a ticket and exorbitant prices for refreshments. We sweat in the heat and humidity. And, likely as not, our team loses. Then we fight the traffic jams on the way home. It makes going to church seem pretty easy, doesn't it?

Faded Memories
of St. Charles

We went back to visit a place that doesn't exist anymore. Reunions are like that. They're like stepping back into a photograph, and for a few hours being there again.

We were high school freshmen in the fall of 1959 at St. Charles College Seminary in Catonsville. Today the buildings are a retirement community, Charlestown. Back then they were a minor seminary, four years of high school and two years of college, preparatory years before entering the major seminary at St. Mary's on Paca Street and in Roland Park.

Ironically, St. Charles, a seminary to prepare men for a celibate life, was located on Maiden Choice Lane.

In reality, more men chose maidens than ever made it to the Catholic priesthood. Of the 105 freshmen who entered that year only seven were ordained. Of those seven priests, two left to marry and one left the Catholic church for a more "conservative" church.

Only 27 of us gathered for the class reunion here in Baltimore a couple of weeks ago. We retold the "war" stories. We remembered 90 beds packed together in dormitories that were too cold in winter and too hot in summer. We remember rigidly scheduled days that began at 5:40 a.m. with prayer, Mass and meditation and ended at 9:30 p.m. with lights out.

The minor seminary was a cross between a military academy and a monastery. Discipline, regimentation and obedience were the core. Studies were hard and intensive. Recreation consisted of organized teams with every person expected to play every sport. Once we arrived in September, we would barely see home again until the following summer.

Once a month we could have visitors. At Christmas and Easter we had a week off. At Thanksgiving and other holidays we had a day off when we who lived locally could go home and bring friends with us.

As the reunion night went on, we repeated old stories about the priests that taught us, their idiosyncrasies and peculiarities. Many of them are deceased now. With a shock many of us realized we were now older than those who had ruled our lives back then.

We remembered our favorite stories about each other. We remembered Dave getting his finger stuck in the sink. We remembered Paul carving chalk figurines during the final study period before our final exams and then flunking out. We remembered Frank who tried to leapfrog over the posts on the tennis court and landed on one. (He prepared for a celibate life the hard way.)

We remembered our cruelties and our kindnesses, and we were both embarrassed and edified.

Then came time for Joe and Dave to bring out their old films. We saw ourselves with red and brown and black hair instead of the gray many of us now wore. We saw thin waists where 30 years later we saw paunches. We saw ourselves as teenagers and realized many of our own children are now older than we were then.

A bit of melancholy was mixed with the shock. There was Ken again. Ken had flown a hundred bombing missions in Vietnam and then was killed on a routine flight to London. Ken was alive again, running and jumping.

There was Mike cutting up and laughing, Mike who had died in an auto accident in Germany. There was another sports hero competing in our track and field events. He had died of AIDS.

When the lights came on again after the films, there were more stories and more cutting up. As we looked at each other, we realized we were the "survivors" of the seminary and of life.

Life had been easy for no one. As one man who had left the seminary after high school put it, "It was like leaving the 13th century and entering the 1960s. I was not prepared for the real world." The seminary's classical education had prepared us well for a world of the past but not world of the future.

Of those at the table who had married, about half were divorced. One had lost his job and had not worked in two years. Most of the others had gone into the helping professions, becoming psychologists, social workers, teachers and administrators in related fields.

All of us had gone different ways in religion, too. One was a Mormon. One had joined another church. The rigidity and discipline of the seminary helped some of us to be daily or weekly Mass attendees. The same rigidity and discipline had so turned others from religion that they had not attended church in 20 years.

The wonderful part of the evening, however, is that no one felt judged or put down. It didn't matter what anyone had done with his life. It mattered that we were there and we were glad to see each other and wanted only the best for each other.

Since we had lived through what often felt like hell, the reunion was a bit of heaven. No guilt. No judgment. No one pretending to be better than anyone else. Just people who had lived through an experience that no one else would ever live again.

Like the characters in the play "Brigadoon," we had stepped into a world that once we left, we could never return to.

All is different now. A housing development now rests on the fields where cows then peacefully grazed at the Wilton Farm Dairy. Today old folks now walk where young folks once ran and played. Maiden Choice Lane remains. There are just fewer choices for the maidens.

Dogs, Cats, Birds & Saints

![]

Some random thoughts about random things:

I think all dog lovers took heart from the scene of Gen. Norman Schwarzkopf arriving home.

Do you remember the scene? It showed the general being greeted by his wife, his children and the family dog. Here was a man who commanded 500,000 of our military personnel, plus coordinated the forces from the 26 coalition countries. And guess what? He couldn't get his dog to sit either!

Speaking of dogs, I heard a veterinarian interviewed recently. He said something very disheartening to dog lovers. In response to a question about whether dogs think they are human, he said, "Dogs don't think they're human. They think of us as dogs. They're pack animals and used to following the leader of the pack."

How discouraging. The next time your dog crawls onto your bed, don't think it's love. He just wants to be close to the leader of the pack.

Lest cat lovers feel left out, I recall a cartoon showing the owner holding Garfield in his lap and saying to him, "There are only two words to describe our relationship – 'unconditional love.'" Meanwhile Garfield is thinking, 'body heat.'

Recently, during a retreat with parents of the handicapped, Sister

Justa Walton told a story of a religion teacher taking her second grade class through the church. She pointed the stained glass windows and talked about the saints pictured there.

Some time later the pastor visited and asked the children if anyone knew what a saint was. A little boy put up his hand and said, "A saint is something that the light shines through." What a wonderful description of a saint – and of Sister Justa.

On the retreat one of the ladies gave Sister Justa a present. The note on the outside of the package read simply, "Now there will be two of you."

Isn't that sweet! Sister thought to herself, I bet there's a little angel in this package.

Instead, when she opened the package there was a little bird inside. "Now there will be two of you" suddenly meant something else. For those who know Sister Justa, she is a bird, but then again, so is the Holy Spirit.

In case you are wondering how bad the season is going for the Orioles, did you hear one of the "highlight" features on WBAL? For non-sports fans, a highlight is a tape of part of the game in which the Orioles do something wonderful. Usually you expect to hear about a home run or a great catch in the field.

This tape clip said:

"Here comes the pitch to Dwight Evans. Ball four! Anderson scores from third." When your highlight is a walk with the bases loaded, you know it's been a tough beginning of the season.

Did you see those two studies? One indicated that men who go to church feel more in control of their lives and have a higher sense of self-esteem. The other study, a much older study, indicated that people who believe in God enjoy sex more than those who don't believe in God. If your parish evangelization committee can advertise that study, people won't walk, they'll run to church. Run announcements of those studies in your parish bulletin, and every Sunday will seem like Christmas.

Perhaps you heard the story of the elderly couple who were just not getting along. The wife begged and begged her husband to go to counseling with her, but the husband always refused. "No counselor is going to tell me what to do," he would say. After many years of asking her husband, the wife said, "OK, I give up. I'll let God settle this."

So the wife paid a visit to church and prayed and prayed for guidance. Finally, she said to God sadly, "Lord, maybe it would be better if you took one of us. Oh, and by the way, Lord, I could live with my sister."

Yes, Sister Justa told that one too.

I'm embarrassed that I can't remember his name, but near the end of April a wonderful man died. He was a good Catholic, a brilliant research scientist, a founder of the St. Thomas Institute in Cincinnati dedicated to higher learning; and when he died, he had over 130 patents. He was a genius, but known more for his products than for his name. What was his most famous invention? Preparation H. When we think of people whose lives made a difference, who relieved pain and brought comfort, we have to remember him.

Two final thoughts:

1) Marriage is the only union that can't be organized. Both sides think they're management.

2) Thou shalt the Sabbath not misuse nor come to church to take thy snooze.

NOVEMBER ▪

Diering Will
Run Forever

■

Was there something almost religious in those mystical, magical moments after the game? What game, you ask?

It seems like a million years ago since the Orioles' last game at Memorial Stadium. A moment of high emotion for fans fades quickly in society's short-term memory.

The quasi-religious moment was in the time at the end of the game. As the music from the "Field of Dreams" played, one by one Orioles from the past began to come onto the field. There were Brooks and Frank. There was Rick Dempsey. There was Jim Palmer.

But as the music continued, there were more and more players, and I felt my eyes filling up with tears and my own emotions tugging at me. I sensed this was more than a good-bye to a stadium or to memories of a team.

It felt like what I imagine our moment of death must be like, a moment in which we see our entire lives being re-run before our eyes. There was Chuck Diering, my favorite player as a child, and suddenly I was nine years old again.

There was Jim Gentile, and I'm in high school and college. There was Boog, and now I'm in the major seminary. And as the players kept pouring onto the field, my life kept passing before me. The young folks behind me probably wondered who this poor sentimental person was. They could see the tears, but they could never understand the feelings.

That memory kept tugging at me through various events. When St. Mary's Seminary and University celebrated 200 years, I wondered what it would be like to see some of the great "stars" from my seminary. To be able to cheer one last time as Father Elmer Putsche jogged onto the field and be in high school again. To feel tears welling up as Father "Pops" Schneider walked onto the field and be in college again. To see Father "Butch" Leigh again and be at St. Mary's Paca Street again.

The more I stayed with the memories of that day at Memorial Stadium, the more I realized that just as I watched my life pass before me, so on the feast of All Saints, the church watches her life pass before her.

For one day, we cheer the great canonized saints: St. Francis of Assisi and St. Clare, for Saints Peter and Paul. We cheer for St. Teresa of Avila and St. Teresa of the Little Flower. We honor those already known to be in heaven's Hall of Fame.

But we also honor those the world has long forgotten. Just as the Chuck Dierings and Gil Coans and Willie Mirandas have faded from the popular mind, so too have millions of faithful people throughout the ages. But if we could assemble humanity and cheer for our real, everyday heroes, would they not include our grandfathers and grandmothers, aunts and uncles, mothers and fathers, the man down the street, the lady next door, the kind teacher, the helpful janitor and all the other real people who make up our everyday life?

In my own mind, like an eternal mantra, I can still hear the voice of Ernie Harwell announcing an Oriole game, "Here comes Diering, rounding third, pulling for the plate. He'll score easily!" In my mind Chuck Diering will run forever, just as he and baseball ran away with a kid's heart back in 1954. But in those same early years, I loved reading the lives of the saints, those heroes of God who also ran away with my heart as a kid.

How Long Does Grief Take?

◼

November is the month of the poor souls. I think it is not just a time to pray for the dead, but also a time to understand a little better some of the grief of the living.

There are a couple aspects of grief that I rarely see addressed, and I would like to reflect on them now. They are first, duration of grief, and second, grief over the death of a brother or sister.

Let's look at duration first.

The book of Ecclesiastes in the Old Testament tells us that there is a time for everything, including a time to grieve. Yet, for all of us that time is different. One of the most helpful things we can do for someone who is grieving is not to set a time limit their grief.

In other words, people will grieve on their own schedules, not on ours.

As I spend time with people who have lost a loved one, I remain amazed at how hurtful some people can be in an effort to be helpful. Well-intentioned friends will say, "Oh, aren't you over that yet?" or "You've got to snap out of it."

Even worse are those who won't even give the bereaved person a chance to talk after a certain period of time.

The greatest gifts we can give to grieving persons is time and non-judgmental listening. They most often don't need our advice on what to do; they need us to reassure them that they will do the right thing.

They don't need us to pressure them into social settings or other gatherings. We may need them to meet someone else, but they may not.

Each person is unique, and each heart has its own time for healing.

In addition to non-judgmental listening, each grieving person can be encouraged to join some kind of grief-support group. There are literally dozens of them available. Such a group can take away that feeling of being in this all alone. A group can reassure a grieving person that others feel or have felt the same way.

Finally, a grieving person can be encouraged to go into counseling. We don't try to operate on ourselves to take out our appendix, but some people think they should remove their own grief.

A good counselor can reduce both the intensity and duration of a person's grief significantly. Catholic Charities and various organizations have such services on a sliding fee scale so that everyone can afford them.

In short, the grieving person deserves our respect, not our judgment. If we really care, we won't limit either the time or the quality of our caring.

In addition to grieving in general, there is a unique kind of grieving over the death of a brother or sister. I'm not aware of much literature in this area. However, it seems to me that the sibling is often neglected in the grieving process.

Much is spoken and written about the loss of a spouse, a parent or a child. Not much is said about the sibling. At the funeral home, great care is usually taken to see that the widow or spouse or child is tended to. What about the brother or sister? Too often they simply move to the background.

Yet, the brother or sister can sometimes be the most significant person in someone's life. During times of marital stress, a brother or sister may even be closer than the spouse.

After the death of a parent, a sister often takes on the role of the family gatherer. For priests especially, a sister is often the most significant family member after the parents die. My sister Helen plays that role in my life.

In this month of November, then, let's pray not only for the dead, but also for greater sensitivity to the living. In fact, the dead may be anything but "poor souls." In the eternal presence of God, they are forever rich. Yet the survivors who grieve alone are poor indeed.

Let's enrich those who mourn with our care and respect. In a special way, let's make an effort to be more sensitive to those who have lost a brother or sister.

Let's do what Christians do so well. Let's notice those whom no one else notices.

Wise Words in the Face of Death

■

Life's greatest wisdom and good advice does not always come from those the world considers brilliant and wise. The best advice most often comes from the simple and unpretentious.

One of the best examples I know happened shortly before Thanksgiving. A family that I have become very close to was coping with the last stages of a mother's terminal illness. Honoring the mother's request to die at home, the father and daughter had around-the-clock care for the mother at home.

As the holidays approached, the daughter said to one of the home care attendants, "Oh, I hope my mother doesn't die on Thanksgiving." The kindly lady said very simply, "Honey, if she does, you just say, 'Thank you, Jesus,' and then you cry."

The mother died just hours past Thanksgiving, but what comfort those words were – "Thank you, Jesus."

Thanks seems a strange thing to say in the face of death, but is it not an appropriate thing for people of faith to say?

We say thanks for this person, for all the good things she experienced and all the good things she shared. We say thanks for the life and goodness that came to us through that person.

We also say thanks that "the strife is o'er, the battle done."

Prolonging biological life, long after any hope of recovery or return of conscious awareness has passed, becomes such a trial to the person and to the loved ones.

To say thanks that the person is now freed from the confines of mortal existence, with all its pains and limitations, and is now freed to be with God in full awareness and peace and joy is indeed something to be profoundly thankful for. It is one of faith's greatest comforts!

As a philosopher once commented, "If you bet there is no God and you win, you win nothing. But if you bet there is a God and you win, you win everything.

For Christians, that is life's safest bet. There is a God, and God is as good as his word.

Beyond saying thanks, there is also the second part of the lady's words, "...and then you cry."

Faith does not deny humanity. Tears are not an indication of a lack of faith. Tears are an indication of our humanity. Faith comforts us with the assurance that our loved one is with God, but tears let us know that we will miss her.

We will be the ones to live with the loss and the emptiness and the change in holiday traditions. At Thanksgiving meals and Christmas celebrations and daily phone calls and other family gatherings, there will be a seat missing, a chair empty, a presence lacking, a voice not spoken.

The funeral liturgy and other prayers at various stations are all meant to give us hope and to help us express our feelings. But faith is still an intellectual concept, and tears come from feelings, our feelings.

I'm never impressed when I hear people try to get other people to deny their feelings by saying things like, "Don't cry. Your mother is with God" or "We're going to smile and be happy at this liturgy because we Christians are Easter people and alleluia is our song."

What nonsense!

No one on earth had greater faith than Jesus of Nazareth, and he saw no contradiction in crying. He cried out on the cross. He cried when his friend Lazarus died. He wept over Jerusalem.

Faith does not replace feelings. After we cope with our feelings of pain and anger and loss and sadness, faith remains to help us to go on.

There are some other words this home care attendant spoke a few weeks earlier. She said, "Some people try to hang on to their loved ones, but the time comes when we need to let them go and give them to God."

Such wise words from a lady with no graduate degrees, no letters after her name, no books to autograph. Just a simple lady who had coped with much personal pain and suffering and who knew how to live and die with faith.

While she did not have the time to read many things, she had read one book quite often – the Bible.

Miracles & the
Limits of Life

Life isn't fair, but God always is. That's a message I've been preaching for many years, but it is not always easy to live, especially when life does not seem fair to us.

Let's look at a specific example. For the past four months I've shared with you stories of my injury to the ligament in my knee. It started from tripping (the first pain was felt in my big toe), but the residual damage was done to my knee. After months of rest, anti-inflammatory drugs (which tore up my stomach) and finally two months of physical therapy, the knee has progressed, but it's not what it was.

Physical therapy has been the "miracle" part of the treatment. What drugs and rest and ice and heat could not accomplish on their own, physical therapy has accomplished through weights and exercises. I've progressed from crutches to cane to limp to walking almost normally.

In my therapist Laura, I have seen the healing power of Christ. Unfortunately, the knee is not perfect. Walking distances and climbing stairs both hurt. And, I think, therein lies the rub for most of us – the miracle versus the limits.

As people of faith, we are called to name life's miracles. As real people, we still mourn life's limits. Let's reflect for a moment on limits and miracles.

Limits are life's realities. People have said to me, "Joe, I know people in their 70s walking fine after an injury, and you're still limping. How come?"

I can only respond, "I know people who are seven feet tall. How come you're not?"

The reality of life is that we don't get equal bodies. Every day I read of people celebrating birthdays in their 80s and other people dropping dead in their 40s. I read of one baby surviving premature birth and another baby dying at birth.

A different doctor or different location or different set of circumstances might make all the difference. However, when we look at life, we are aware that we don't get the same health, the same brains, the same opportunities.

Limits are not much fun, but they are life's realities. We can choose to get angry, to get depressed, to get bitter, but life still does not change much. We might well wish life had dealt us another hand, but all we can realistically do is to play the hand life has dealt us. At our birth, God didn't give us a warranty on parts or life duration.

Fortunately, God gave us something better. God has given us his own presence. As I say on the radio, God never promised us a rose garden, but he did promise to stay with us.

That's why I think we need, as people of faith, to see the presence of God wherever it is. When Jesus hung on the cross, he seemed pretty abandoned by God, didn't he? Yet, there was his mother, his apostle John, a few women.

In life, we can mourn what we do not have, mourn those who have left us and fail to see God in what we have. That's why I can see God in my physical therapist Laura, for "the lame are walking."

We need to see God in the speech therapist who helps the child or stroke victim to speak, "for the dumb are speaking." We need to see God when an individual or team resuscitates a person, "for the dead are being raised to life."

We need to see God in the surgeon performing the delicate operation on someone's eyes, "for the blind are seeing." In short, we need to look for the presence of God when we are tempted to look just at the limits of life.

Maybe we lost a knee or a job or some money or a relationship. We have a right to mourn, and we need time to come to terms with life's realities. But we have not lost God, and God won't lose us.

Ultimately, we need to celebrate God's greatest miracle – the resurrection. In the funeral Mass is that wonderful line, "Life is changed, not ended." Life is changed by every loss, every death; but it is changed, not ended.

After each of life's little deaths is another resurrection. After an injury, we can learn to get around in a new way. After a job loss, we can discover another way to make a living. After the loss of a relationship, we can find a new relationship or come to a new appreciation of our singleness.

There is always life after death. Life is not fair, but God always is. God transforms life's limits. One day God will even transform our ultimate limit of mortality into everlasting life with him.

That's God's promise, and God keeps his promises.

Thanks to All
the Good Parents

■

I just wanted to thank all the good parents of the world.

Every day in my roles as priest, confessor and counselor, I see some of the most hurting people in the world. Very often these are the people with childhood memories of being abandoned, abused, neglected or just ignored.

The theme that seems to connect their lives is low self-esteem resulting from deprivation of love in their early lives. So I just felt the need to tell all of you good parents – who gave love, who did not abandon, neglect or abuse your children – what great people you are.

Perhaps we hear too many stories of the tragedies of life, and we don't pay enough attention to all the good that is done every day. The moment this struck me was when I was doing the "intake" (gathering background information) from a client just beginning counseling. This person was coming not with personal problems but with some relation-ship questions.

The information I was gathering was so different from what I was used to hearing. Here was a young man who had happy memories of childhood.

He remembered enjoying his brothers and sisters as they grew up. He remembered Mom and Dad as having enough love and enough time to make each child feel special. He showed good self-esteem, success on his job and a general acceptance of himself as he was.

I just had the urge to call his parents to tell them what a good job they had done. Since I could not violate the counselor-client confidentiality, I thought I would write this general article instead.

So often good parents do not give themselves the credit they deserve. They know their own shortcomings and how imperfect their home life is. Yet I always hasten to comfort parents with the thought that if they were perfect parents, they wouldn't be preparing their children for the real world.

The world is not perfect. These parents are showing children that they can be imperfect and still be loved.

A second thing good parents tend to do is to blame themselves, to take too much responsibility for what their adult children do with their lives. Parents often berate themselves when an adult child gets pregnant or gets someone else pregnant out of wedlock, when an adult child abuses drugs or alcohol, when a child gets divorced.

It's very important for parents to know that however good and loving they are, they are not the only influence on their children's lives. A whole host of things, from the media to peer pressure to a hedonistic culture, will exert influences on all of us.

One thing parents can take comfort in is that adults raised with love in a stable home tend to "recover" much more easily.

With a good sense of self-esteem from a loving childhood, these are the people most likely to do the responsible thing when faced with a pregnancy, to profit most from drug and alcohol rehabilitation programs and to be able to profit from counseling and make a better marital choice in the future.

In other words, people with self-esteem from childhood tend to be able to stop destructive behavior rather than repeating self-defeating "life scripts" that they may have learned in childhood.

A young mother recently told me a story that seems to encapsulate so much of what I have been saying. Her little 2 1/2-year-old had just awakened from his nap. She gave him some juice and gently helped him back to consciousness. She asked him, "Is there anything you want?" Sleepily he replied, "I just want some love." So she spent the next 15 minutes holding him and snuggling with him.

Without her realizing it, I think she was building up an "emotional bank account" for him that he will draw on for years to come. Years from now, when the incident is long forgotten, he will know that life can be good and that he is lovable. Parenthood can be a taken-for-granted occupation. Children don't say thanks very often. I just wanted to thank you on behalf of your children. Your love makes a difference. I see it all the time.

DECEMBER ■

When Father
Comes to Dinner

During the Christmas season, many parishioners want to share their family joy by inviting a priest to dinner. It's an ancient custom, not as old as bringing home the Yule log, but sometimes just as challenging. In order to help individuals and families avoid some of the pitfalls of this practice, I am here reprinting my "Home Rules for Feeding Priests:"

1. Never invite two priests to the same meal. Probably one reason why a priest would accept an invitation to dinner would be to get away from eating with other priests for a change.
2. At dinner, never mention all the other priests you have had to dinner. Every priest likes to feel unique. He doesn't like to feel like one more stamp in your collection.
3. Never compliment the priest by comparing him with someone else. For example, never say, "Oh, Father X, you are so wonderful. You remind us of Father Y." Father X may not feel complimented. He might think that Father Y doesn't play with a full deck. He may then start doubting your judgment of him.

4. Conversely, any comparison with God is always acceptable. For example, "Father, you remind me so much of Jesus" is always in good taste. Children should also be coached not to ask an embarrassing question like, "Are you as old as God?"
5. While comparison with God is always commendable, occasionally comparison with one of the apostles is acceptable. For example, "Father, you remind me of James the Less."
6. Pay no attention to Father's manners. If you're hung up on manners, you should have invited Ricardo Montalban or Charlie Eckman.
7. If you ask Father to dinner and he refuses, be complimented, not put down. He must think a great deal of you to be honest with you.
8. Start worrying if half an hour after he arrives, he excuses himself and says, "I hate to eat and run, but I have a wake service at six o'clock." There are no wake services at six o'clock.
9. Never tell him your problems at dinner or bring up problems of the parish. Instead, ask him about his problems, and if you're lucky, he'll tell you. That way you'll get a chance to experience what he goes through all day.
10. Never offer a priest any alcoholic beverage. Priests don't drink. Occasionally, one or two may imbibe a Dr. Pepper or Chocolate Yoo-Hoo.
11. Don't be offended if later that same evening you see Father coming out of the Pizza Hut. Priests often take the youth group out for snacks.
12. If your children ask Father to play a game with them after dinner, make sure they understand the ground rules: They are supposed lose.
13. Don't be offended if Father stayed longer at someone else's house. Just keep telling yourself, "They must have more problems than we do."
14. If Father starts telling you his seminary stories, interrupt by reminding him that this is the evening your family practices its home fire drill.

15. If you were kind and it's now 3 a.m. and all of you have your pajamas on and the dog is snoring under the coffee table and there's a pattern staring back from the television and Father is still telling his seminary stories, don't be offended. You've got a friend.

What the Police
Are Guilty Of

It was like a scene from a movie. There was the police car, parked by the side of the road, lights flashing, while the officer inside tried to write up a traffic ticket. In front was a car with expired tags, the reason for the ticket.

Next to the car stood a distraught young mother with her two children. Her 5-year-old son kept asking, "Mommy, are you going to get arrested? Mommy, are you going to jail?" The little 3-year-old girl kept running up to the police car, waving to the officer and repeating, "Merry Christmas. Happy New Year. Merry Christmas. Happy New Year."

The police officer writing the ticket seemed to be sinking lower in his seat. Finally, he got out of his car and said to the mother, "Look, lady, when a car has expired tags, I'm supposed to take off the tags and have it towed. That's at least a $90 charge for you. I'm not going to do that, but I do have to give you this ticket. Be careful driving home."

When the woman explained the complications involved in her life at that time, the officer added, "Why don't you go to court? You might get off."

A couple of days later as the mother was leaving her home, the same police officer happened to be driving past. He spotted her and stopped, "I'm sorry I had to give you that ticket the other day. I hope you'll go to court. You might get off. "

I tell that story because it never made the headlines. No one videotaped it. No one talked about it on talk shows. The police chief was not praised for it.

Regulations were not followed. A citizen was not treated according to the letter of the law. A citizen was treated better than the law.

I believe that scene is repeated thousands of times in a variety of ways. A cop gives a kid a break. A stranded motorist is helped. Police men and women on and off duty go the extra mile to help someone.

Few people talk about those scenes. Few police are publicly indicted for acts of kindness. Juries are not selected to praise loyalty and dedication and service beyond the call of duty. Headlines will be fueled with efforts to convict a few police officers for their crimes.

Do we not have an equal obligation to convict the vast majority of police for their goodness?

Crossing the Deserts
In Our Lives

■

Do you have a camel in your life?

No, not the kind that you would walk a mile to smoke, but the symbolic camel in your character that helps you cross the deserts and dry spells of life.

Let me explain this by quoting Carlos Velles, S.J.: "Tagore says that we all need a camel in our lives. A horse is fine for beauty and strength and speed and breed, to enjoy a ride and run a race and win a prize. All very fine. But then there are deserts also in life and there the best of horses is of no use and speed is of no avail.

"The horse will grow impatient and restless and its hoofs will sink in the sand and its breath will burn in the heat and it will run wild and fall and die in the ruthless sand. Horses are not for deserts.

"But camels are. The camel will set on its route and will keep on and on and on. Even without food, without water, without reins, without directions, it will go on steadily, faithfully, reliably, and it will keep its course and cross the desert and reach the waters and save itself and its rider.

"The dogged perseverance to keep to one's course steadily in the worst circumstances is a prized asset for survival in this world. We all need a camel in our stables."

As we reach for an Advent or Christmas meditation, might we not do well to think of the three astrologers, the wise men from the East? Usually they are pictured as riding camels. Can they not be symbols for our life's journey?

Look at all the astrologers experienced.

First, they experienced betrayal at the hands of political authorities. King Herod gave them assistance only because he hoped to get an opportunity to kill the child they sought.

Second, and far worse, their innocent asking for directions resulted in wholesale slaughter of all children under the age of two. Did they not have some doubts about their own wisdom?

Third, would not their following the star have cost them something? To go in search is also to leave something else behind. Were they mocked by their neighbors, scorned by their peers and questioned by their own families?

Fourth, they knew the humiliation of getting lost. The star that guided their journey evidently disappeared. Did they doubt their own sanity, their own faith, their own notion of God?

Finally, they got their bearings again and found Christ.

What kept the astrologers going? Was it not both the camels they rode and the camels within them? Can we not identify with the need for such camels in our lives?

Have we not all had the experience of having our faith betrayed, of being let down by people we thought we could trust? People who have lost a job, lost a marriage through divorce or lost their self esteem through some kind of abuse – all these people can understand the wise men.

Have we not had some of our best efforts turn into disasters? Have we not all had the experience of being misunderstood, of having our motives held suspect, of having our efforts to help turn into hurtful experiences?

People who have had a baby die of Sudden Infant Death Syndrome or had a loved one die by suicide know that the story of the Holy Innocents and that senseless deaths go on even today.

Have we not all had to pay a price to follow our dreams? Maybe we chose a lower-paying job in order to do more for others and now realize how little appreciated our sacrifice was. Maybe we elected to teach in a parochial school and now experience much lower income and much less retirement security than we might have had if we had gone into a public system.

Maybe we chose to be a priest or nun, to follow a dream of leaving all to follow Christ, and now wonder what our lives mean in a secular society that little understands such choices and respects them even less. Maybe we chose to have the "extra" baby or chose our family over a promotion at work and now we know what following our dream has cost us.

Have we had the experience of getting lost? Have the stars that guided our lives in youth and young adulthood become lost in the clouds of daily life? Have we broken our promises, lowered our standards, compromised our values? Can we accept, like the wise men, that God loves us for our faithfulness to the journey and that he forgives our failures along the way?

Finally, like the astrologers, can we believe that we will find Christ at the end of our journey? In the words of the Negro spiritual, can we believe that "God didn't bring us this far to leave us now?"

With our eyes on the goal, our choices make sense. So let's call on the camel within us to help us stay committed in our marriages, faithful in our religious choices, loyal to spiritual values.

The Magi had two essentials: the camel and a star. We need love and a dream. The camel becomes the enduring love, the tough love, the faithful love for God that keeps us going through life's desert. The star is our dream, the guiding light, the golden rule, the purpose for our existence.

If we can keep a camel in our lives, then we will be able to keep Christmas all the days of our lives.

What God Looks Like

Christmas is about the color of God. Christmas is about the God who comes in stables and emergency rooms to show us what God looks like. The stable story we know pretty well. The emergency room story is personal. Allow me to tell it.

Recently, I was back in the emergency room because of my knee. (Yes, the knee that just won't heal after two months of medication and therapy.)

I was accompanied by a good friend of mine who is both an orthopedic nurse and pregnant. As we sat in what seemed like the Waiting Room for Hell, I commented, "Mag, I bet we're creating a few conversations today. A priest seated next to a pregnant woman. They're probably wondering which of us is in more trouble."

Then I became more Christmasy. "You know, this is like the first Christmas. You're Margaret Mary, and I'm Joseph. You're pregnant, and I had nothing to do with it. And there's no room for us in the inn."

Eventually I was called for treatment, and while I was examined, given crutches and more medication, I overheard a conversation in the next cubicle. A young boy of African-American descent was getting some stitches in his leg. As the doctor sewed the boy up, she chatted with him. "Do you see the yellowish tissue? Do you know what that is?" she asked.

"No," the boy replied.

"That's fat," the doctor replied. "It comes from eating too much junk food." The doctor then laughed and continued, "I know because I have too much of the same stuff in me."

She then uttered those simple and profound closing words, "On the inside we all look exactly the same."

I realized at that moment that while I had temporarily lost a knee, I had found again the meaning of Christmas. In this strange world of sick people and bruised and torn bodies and forms to be filled and bureaucratic procedures to be followed – into this world there quietly stepped the presence of God.

At Christmas we celebrate the God who came looking like us so that we would all know that we looked like God.

In the "real" world, like Martha in the Scriptures, we are all busy about many things. We are patients or care providers, consumers or donors, customers or employees, hurting or happy, awake or asleep.

And into our world, which is often too busy to notice, God enters just as God entered another world too busy to notice 2,000 years ago. But the mystery of Christmas is that there is no mystery at all.

God is always all around us, sometimes in those comforting us and in those needing comfort, sometimes in those happy who want to share joy and sometimes in the sorrowing who wait for others to care. Christmas is the one-day celebration of the God here all days.

A closing story. A little boy told his mother that he was going to draw a picture of God. As he started drawing, his mother replied, "Honey, you can't do that. No one knows what God looks like." With all the confidence in the world, the boy replied, "They will when I get finished."

Somehow I imagine another somewhat similar conversation between a heavenly father and another son.

I imagine the father saying, "No one knows what God looks like." And the son, as he steps across the stars from eternity to time, from heaven to earth, responds, "They will when I get finished."

The Last
Reindeer Visit

Most reindeer pull sleighs, but this one was along for the ride. Wrapped in Christmas paper, he sat on the seat next to the priest.

It was a pleasant ride this Christmas eve. The evening Masses were finished, and after he had greeted the crowds of people that mobbed the church, it was pleasant to ride through the quiet night. All the radio stations were playing Christmas carols.

However, except for an occasional patch of fog on one of the valley roads this mild winter night, there would be no other white stuff for Christmas.

Within a short time, the priest and the reindeer arrived at Stella Maris Hospice. The halls and rooms were decorated with lights, tinsel and trees. A few flights up and the priest and the reindeer were in the hospice unit. On this night when the world celebrated a birth, the priest would visit his mother awaiting death.

After some hugs and kisses, it was time to present the gift. Unwrapping the paper, she hugged her reindeer.

With his tiny antlers and floppy legs, he could easily be mistaken for a dog. He soon was. A nurse's aide asked, "Is that a dog?"

"No," she said proudly, "this is a reindeer."

As the aide left the room, the mother continued with mock surprise,

"Imagine. Confusing my reindeer with a dog!"

The three of them sat quietly and talked softly as the sound of Christmas music wafted through the halls.

As she held the reindeer, he remembered the times when she had held him. On her lap as a child, he had first learned of reindeer flying and sleighs being pulled.

In her arms he had heard of a wonderful person called Santa Claus who had driven that sleigh from rooftop to rooftop delivering presents. Together they had listened to the song of another reindeer named Rudolph who had risen above the taunts of his fellow reindeer to save another foggy Christmas with his shiny nose.

Far more important, from her he had learned of a far greater story. He had heard the story of a God who became man and who was born of poor parents in a stable.

In his childhood days he had frankly found more comfort in the story of Jesus' birth than in the story of Santa Claus. Growing up poor, he had never shared the bounty of this Santa Claus the way others did, but learning that Jesus was poor made him feel good.

He could identify with this Jesus, and he suspected that Jesus understood him. It was this kind of identification that would lead him to stop by his parish church on Christmas night many years before.

In those days when churches were still left unlocked, he could sit in a dark church or kneel in front of a lighted stable and see the poor God who loved poor people.

Perhaps it was this understanding of God coming for others that would lead him to become a priest who would bring God to others in the form of bread and wine.

Soon it was time to go, and with a kiss for his mother and a pet for the reindeer, he was off. The sounds of holiday joy melted in the air, but sadness touched his heart. As he drove away, he knew with the certainty of Santa driving his sleigh into the night that the last reindeer had visited his mother on her last Christmas.

Today that reindeer stares down from his perch on the bookshelf at the priest at his desk working on his writings. From his perch amidst the other decorations, he stands as a guardian of past Christmas traditions and past Christmas memories.

From her place in another realm of time and space, that mother now watches all reality beneath her.

Beneath her, Santa and his sleigh again circle the world. Beneath her a Christmas star shines.

Beneath her, a troubled couple searches for lodging.

Beneath her, God is born again on earth as Scriptures are explained and bread is broken.

And as this mother watches over her son, she watches another Mother watch over another Son. Christmas comes again, and the last reindeer flies forever.

Lights That Show the Way Through January's Nights

As the cold winter nights of January cover our land, I yearn nostalgically for the lights of Christmas. For you who may be looking at your gas and electric bills and wondering why you bothered to decorate, allow me to say a belated word of thanks. Let me offer a few reasons for my thankfulness.

First, the lights you put up at Christmas gave hope to the world. Contrast the emptiness and darkness of January with the warm sparkling decorations of the holidays, and you know what I mean. Christians, if we are nothing else, are meant to be signs of hope. We have faith that Christ is the light of the world, and he brought a light that the darkness could not overcome.

In January, however, we face a tougher challenge. Instead of stringing lights on a tree or house to let them shine, we must be lights in our world. "Let your good deeds be seen so that they may give thanks to our Father in heaven."

Second, a light, no matter how small, pierces the darkness. I'm always touched by the single candle in a window, often an apartment window in a poor section of town. That single wreath with its candle may be all that person or family can afford.

Growing up in poverty, when we could afford no more, the little candle always shone at Christmas. It is forever a symbol of the David of light conquering the Goliath of the darkness. A person with faith lights the candle to put darkness in its place.

As Father Blair Raum has said so eloquently, "A person filled with fear could look at Goliath and say, 'He's too big to fight!' A person with faith could look at Goliath and say, 'He's too big to miss.'" The smallest light defeats the greatest darkness.

A third reason for gratefulness for the lights of Christmas is that they show the power of goodness. We have all heard the old expression that "Evil will win as long as good people are content to do nothing." The darkness of January lets us see what happens when we do nothing. But the lights of the holidays show how a combined effort to do good literally changes a dreary world into a winter wonderland. That's the power of human goodness. What an eloquent reminder of the Christopher motto, "Better to light one candle than curse the darkness." The world will never be lacking in darkness to curse. Unfortunately, the cursing compounds the darkness. But light scatters the darkness, hence the power of goodness.

And remember, the greatest galaxy of lights is no more than a combination of individual lights. It is never the magnitude of the good deed that matters. As Mother Teresa so eloquently put it, "We are not called to do great things but to do small things with great love."

So the lights of Christmas are all packed away now in their cartons, but let's not pack away our capacity to be lights in our world. Fear says, "Don't go out at night." But those Christmas lights remind us that we can walk the streets and sing carols. Faith can reclaim what fear surrenders. So "let's set aside deeds of darkness and put on the armor of light." How our world needs people of the light!

About the Author

Father Joseph Breighner continues to write his weekly column on religion and life for *The Catholic Review* newspaper. His weekly half-hour radio show, *Country Roads*, is nationally syndicated. He travels extensively offering workshops, recollection meetings, and weekend retreats. Ordained in 1971, he served as a parish minister for six years and then as the Coordinator of Evangelization for the Archdiocese of Baltimore. Currently, he is working as a pastoral counselor and spiritual director. He is the author of *Reflections From the Country Road*, *Seeking Serenity*, and *Does It All Makes Sense*.